Blanche Fearing

In the City by the Lake

In Two Books

Blanche Fearing

In the City by the Lake
In Two Books

ISBN/EAN: 9783744708746

Printed in Europe, USA, Canada, Australia, Japan

Cover: Foto ©Thomas Meinert / pixelio.de

More available books at **www.hansebooks.com**

IN THE CITY BY THE LAKE.

Here in this splendid city by the lake,
I dream that man has a majestic hope,
Because all elements of life and thought
Enrich her blood and stimulate her brain.
Here is the world epitomized, for here
Are pulses out of every nation's heart,
And men may study mankind at their hearths.
This is to be a favorite battle-ground
For truth and error. Here, as time moves on,
Great causes will be marshaled. Times have been
Already, when the stirring trumpet blast
Of an approaching conflict, shook the world
Out of its dream of safety. Oh, then teach
All capable of bearing the bright arms
Of reason, fearless, independent thought!
If you would lead men surely angelward,
Teach them to think,—not what to think, but how.

IN THE CITY BY THE LAKE

IN TWO BOOKS

THE SHADOW, AND THE SLAVE GIRL

BY

BLANCHE FEARING,

Author of "The Sleeping World," Etc.

CHICAGO:
SEARLE & GORTON
1892

TO MY SISTER,
MARIEN E. FEARING

CONTENTS

BOOK I.—THE SHADOW.

    PART 1. LOVE   11

    PART 2. LIFE   28

    PART 3. DEATH   53

    PART 4. RESURRECTION   71

BOOK II.—THE SLAVE GIRL.

    PART 1. FREEDOM   95

    PART 2. SLAVERY   108

    PART 3. REVOLT   130

    PART 4. FREEDOM REGAINED   167

BOOK I
THE SHADOW

PART I

LOVE

There is a splendid city by a lake
That beats against its sea-wall restlessly,
Like a great heart that hungers;—ever beats
With mournful, mystic music, as if chafed
By a great nameless sorrow;—beats and beats,
As if the secret heart-aches of all hearts
That ever in that city beat and break,
Were buried in it. Almost it would seem,
Some great magician plied his magic art
To build that city, for so swift it raised
Its domes, and towers, and spires to the sun,
Far swifter than the slowly-building hand
Of man is wont to raise them. Up it sprang,
Most like the phantom fabric of a dream.
One day a lonely fort 'mid savage tribes
Who scudded through the waving prairie grass
After the deer and bison; and the next,
A little village cradled by a lake
That sang to it its solemn old sea-song,
With but a handful of men's souls; the next,
A busy town, an infant Hercules
Among earth's splendid cities, even then,
In sturdy childhood, giving prophecy

Of giant labors to be wrought; to-day,
A mighty city, and the whole world hears
Its roaring wheels of commerce, and its din
Of flying shuttles and of thunderous looms,
Fierce heart-throbs of its mighty engines driven
By the white steeds of lightning and of steam,
Whose splendid pulses to the borders roll;—
A city whose own breath has dimmed the sun.
And once a flying fiend of fire swept,
With lurid wings and blasting, stifling breath,
Across the city, and behold, a heap
Of dully glowing embers where it stood.
Again the great magician plied his art—
The spirit of the new age—and again
That city raised its gleaming domes and spires
To greet the early kisses of the sun.
Now men who cannot prick their slower brains
Up to the dizzy speed of life and thought
That through the streets upon the whirling car
Of progress, thunder, rub their eyes and gasp,
As if, like Rip Van Winkle, they had slept
For twenty years, "Ah! pray, what doth it mean?
Why, here we had a village yesterday!"

Out of the city's hot, tumultuous heart,
Just out of sound of the fierce hum and hiss
Of human insects spinning their cocoons,
His little world of interest, each for self,
To bury himself in it, and the buzz
Of golden honey-makers, 'round one flower,
A thousand swarming for its poison sweets;—

Just out of sound of these lived Robert Earle,
A quiet, courtly man, who, having stored
Enough of golden honey, had withdrawn
Into his princely hive to live upon it,
With his one child, a daughter, Edith Earle.
He, in his youth, against the wish and will
Of all his kindred, had been early wed
Unto a simple maiden, who had naught
To recommend her but a brave, true heart,
Revealed within a sweetly serious face,
As clearly as the silver sands that lie
At bottom of a lucid mountain lake.
So deep and constant was his love for her,
That when she died at end of three bright years,
And left him with a helpless babe, he kept
Her memory like a fragrance in his heart,
As if an angel, stooping, plucked a rose
Out of his bosom, but the perfume rare
Lingered through all life's garments, sweetening all.
"Edith, my rose!" he called her in her life;
Nor thought nor wish had he to wed again,
No love but for his child—his child and hers.
Now all of joy and hope and loveliness
That wealth of gold and wealth of love could give
To make life beautiful, to her were given;
And little Edith had her mother's heart,
As well as violet eyes and shining hair,
And more—the careful culture of the mind.
All rapturously the father watched his bud
Unfolding into girlhood's radiant rose.
"Edith, my rose!" he cried in clasping her—

"My rose without a thorn!" and kissed her cheek,
First one and then the other, each a rose,
And then the mouth, a rosebud in between,
And then the forehead, like a snow-white dove
Outgleaming from its nest of shining curls,
And had no thought, no heart for aught but her,
Except one friend, the comrade of his youth
And later life.   Between these two had grown
A friendship that had ripened with the years
Into a noble intimacy.   He,
Like Robert Earle, possessed an only child,
The rosy star of his declining years.
Now Lucius was a bright, gay, handsome youth
A little rollicking but honorable,
With kindly, courteous ways and easy grace
That won all hearts, and pleased his father well.
Now Robert Earle and Arthur Coventry
Spoke much about the children, till it came
To be the cherished idol of their hearts
That they should love each other, and then wed.
"Nothing by force!" said Robert, "we will sow
The precious seed, then nurse the tender plant
With gentle words of praise like summer dew,
And sweet companionship like summer sun."
So played the children, and the fathers smiled,
And so the rosy hours of childhood flew,
Like birds of passage, and were lost to sight,
Far in the dim, blue distance of the past.
All rapturously the father watched his bud
Unfolding into girlhood's radiant rose,
And had no thought, no heart for aught but her;

And Edith loved her father ardently.
In him was childhood's playmate, girlhood's friend,
Father and mother, almost lover he.

It chanced upon a night, (we say it chanced,
Nor know if it be chance, or if, indeed,
An unseen tether to a hand divine,
Draw us so gently this way, that we go,
Unconscious of the leading) a June night,
That Edith met, as any one might meet,
In all this labyrinth of human ways
Where footpaths meet and cross, and meet no more,
A quiet, sober man, a modest clerk
In a great merchant house; young, but he seemed
Older by ten years than in truth he was,
For his had been a lonely, thoughtful life.
Years make not old, but only thought that is
The ripening frost of the eternal. Lo,
Over the life of Walter Gray there flushed,
On that June night, a color and a glow,
When Edith Earle broke on him like the morn,
A rosy light between monotonous hills
Of toil and duty, till they burned and glowed
Like colored altar-fires by angels fed.
Day after day caught up the rosy light,
And flashed it kindling on from day to day,
As morning beam is flashed from peak to peak,
When, 'neath the white feet of the morning star,
The crimson billows of the day surge up.
A sudden inspiration filled his life,
As when one turns the leaves of some old book,

And stumbles on a poem suddenly,
That flames afresh life's purpose in his soul.
So, slowly turning o'er the thumb-worn leaves
Of life's prosaic book with weary hands,
He stumbled on this poem—Edith Earle;
And all his thoughts ran into rhythmic words,
And set themselves to music in his brain.
For what is poetry but that which gives
A glory and divineness unto things
Of common names and uses? Men and women,
Who set us palpitating with the thrill
Of something loftier than we yet have dreamed,
Are God's sublimest poems.
       Edith Earle
Felt in her life a sudden strength and breadth,
A deepening downward toward unsounded depths,
A lifting upward toward unmeasured heights;
And all her soul shook out its gleaming sails,
And through them blew a fresh, strong breath of life,
Which brought her to a new mysterious world;
As one, who, sailing on familiar seas,
And carried by a fresh wind from his course,
Is startled by an undiscovered land.
How is it that one human soul draws out
Another's grace and power, where a third
Can find no strength or sweetness, as the sun
Brings out the flush and flavor of the fruit
From which the moonlight draws no taste or tint?
Edith kept this first secret of her life
Unshared with him who shared all things beside,
And kept it through no fear or bashfulness,

But through the wonder of it;—it seemed so strange,
As if a waiting angel stretched his hand
Just at the moment when the soul was right,
And touched a secret spring that opened wide
A mystic chamber that was unforeguessed;
And all her words and actions grew subdued,
As if to keep the music in her heart,
As a musician sometimes muffles up
The instrument to keep the music in.
Now Robert Earle looked wise, and in his heart
Shook hands with Cupid, smiling, but spoke not.
So, like a serpent taking tail in mouth,
Completed was the circle of the year,
Whose end and whose beginning met in June.

After the first sweet rapture of it all,
A trouble thrust itself in Walter's heart,
And beat there like a heart within a heart;
And sometimes he would clasp his hands upon it,
As if to ease it, for it seemed a thing
So tangible, it ached and quivered so.
Once in that second June he said to her:
"Edith, my heart is troubled; I must speak.
However hard the doing of a thing,
'Tis easier done than thought of night and day.
I do but wrong you with this love of mine.
Why should I love you—I, who am so poor
In all those things which make life pleasurable?
You have been used to costly robes and gems
And fairy laces, and those lily hands
Were never soiled with labor. This will change,

Unless we be your father's pensioners,
Which never can be. I but do you wrong
To link your life with mine, and mar it so."
Then Edith turned upon him with her face
Flushed like the sunrise, answering, "I do pray
No darker trouble ever come to you,
My Walter. When I was a little child,
And my good nurse would clothe my baby limbs
In costly garments, I would run away,
And find my father, sobbing piteously,
'My father, take them off—I cannot play.'
I like the best to wear a simple dress,
And only wear the costlier ones to please
My father, who delights to see me clad
In beautiful garments. True, these idle hands
Have never learned to toil, but I am strong;
I hate the ease and languor of my life,
And it will be a joy to strive with you,
To brave the things that other hearts have braved,—
So taste the life most men and women live.
My father shall not help his children more
Than fathers help their children commonly.
O Walter, we are both so young and strong!"
She paused all breathless, for the hurrying words
Had tripped each other, coming tremulously,
As if each had a heart that beat too fast;
And such a high, sweet courage lit her face,
A tender mist came over Walter's eyes.
He knew her maiden fancy tinged the truth,
But had no heart to tell her, for she looked
So flushed and splendid, so he only gazed,

And almost worshiped her.   Instinctively
We bow the head before the soul that dares.
"Another thing"—he said, "have you no dread
Of his, your father's anger?" Edith smiled:
"My father never yet has frowned on me;
He never crossed my will in anything;
To make me happy is his happiness,
But I will tell him of it now, this night."

So Edith came and laid her shining head
Against her father's knee, and clasped his hand,
And looking up with her frank, fearless gaze,
She said, "My father, I have kept too long
My secret; I have loved now for a year."
Then Robert Earle brushed something large and
    bright,
That like a jewel rolled down from his cheek,
And laid a hand upon the shining head:
"My daughter does but share the common fate,
For every one will have his time to love
As surely as he has his time to die.
And does he love my rose? But wherefore ask?
Could any help it, being loved by her?"
"He loves me, father."
                      "Where is he—the rogue!
Why comes he not to ask my blessing? Go,
And send for Lucius; tell him I would see him."
Then Edith looked aghast, and all the rose
Died from her cheek, like sunset from the west
When suddenly a cloud drops down the sky.
"It is not Lucius that I love—no, no!

My father, you have never seen his face."
The hand slipped downward from the shining head.
For the first time in all her whole sweet life,
Her father frowned upon her, and she drooped.
"Edith, why have you kept this thing so long?
This surely is a fancy that will flit
Across your brain, and leave it clear again."
He pushed her from him, clinging to his knees,
And, rising, paced the room three times, then turned,
Saying, "Go bring him to me, and I swear
To bless you both, if he be worthy of you."
Again he paced the room, and shook his head,
And muttered to himself, "What cursèd fools
Men are when they adjudge themselves most wise."
Meanwhile came Edith to where Walter stood,
Leaning against a pillar of the porch.
She said, "He asks to see you, Walter, come!"
And Walter followed her, as one who goes
To meet his doom. One's seldom at his best,
Feeling himself on trial. He only does
His noblest in the sweet unconsciousness
Of observation. Walter never missed
His manly poise so far as on that night.
He sat uneasily upon his chair,
And plucked his fingers, groping through his words,
And almost felt the manhood in him die;
And, feeling that he shamed her he loved most,
Was thrice unmanned; but Robert Earle was cool
And critical, probing calmly, point by point,
His mind and prospects, noticed every flaw,
Without discriminating between those

Which were by nature and by habit wrought
Into the substance, and those which were made
Upon the surface, idle finger marks
Of the occasion, to be brushed away
By the next happier moment. When at last,
The trial ended, the accused dismissed,
Came Edith in her fleecy robe of white,
And nestled like a lamb between his knees,
Who dropped his withered hands like autumn leaves
Upon the golden summer of her hair.
She, thinking to herself that he had seen
The manhood through the moment's awkwardness,
Let her sad heart beat lighter. Then he spoke:
"Edith, my rose, he is not worthy of you,
Has neither personal grace nor gifts of mind —
A stupid, penniless fellow, who but seeks
To make his own nest soft with others' down.
Wake from this dream!—he is not worthy of you."
She drew away from his caressing touch.
"You shall not speak so, father; you have heard
How any one may wear a guilty look,
When put upon his trial; and besides,
No man was ever seen alike by two.
My nature has a side for every friend;
No one may stand upon a middle height,
And view the complex whole. Do you not know
We often seem least noble in the hour
When we would seem our noblest? Furthermore,
We see the thing we seek for, good or ill,
Far easier than the thing we would not see.
You should not judge him, knowing him one hour;

You should believe me who have had a year
For passing judgment." Robert Earle looked down
Into the glowing face upturned to him,
And, like an angel gleam in every look
And queenly motion, saw her mother's soul,
But stronger, loftier, and set himself,
With all his strength of will, against the man,
Who dared to win her heart, while being so far
Unworthy of her, and the ominous clouds
Began to gather on his brow; the smile
Died down upon his lips, and left them dark.
"Take a month, Edith—think of it a month."
"My father, I have thought of it a year."
  But take another month now that you know
My heart is set against it, and he seems
To me unworthy of you, for you know
That you are all I have on earth to love."
He motioned, and she rose and sadly went.

In those dark days of coldness and restraint,
The first between them, Sorrow first appeared—
Sorrow, who never slighted human heart,—
And touched her, shrinking. Walter shook his head,
Saying in sadness, "He will never yield."
But Edith answered, "Walter, never fear,
Because he loves me so."
                        Now when a month,
A golden wheel that forward bears the year
Upon its circle, turned upon itself,
Came Edith in a fleecy robe of white,
And nestled like a lamb between his knees,

Who laid a hand upon her shining head:
"Edith, my rose, speak, tell me that this dream
Has vanished in the light of sober thought."
She answered softly: "Learn to love?—not hard;
Unlearn it?—surely God can unmake souls
Most easier than we do that, being true.
I am not dreaming, therefore cannot wake."
"Take a month, Edith, take another month,
Then come again, and speak the final word;
Remember you are all I have on earth."
He motioned, and she rose and sadly went.
"Edith, I know that he will never yield,"
Said Walter Gray, and sadly shook his head.
"And if he will not, Walter, we will wed,
And when 'tis done past all undoing, then
I know he will relent, and bless us both—
He loves me so!"
     So slipped another month,
Wanting yet two nights only.   Walter walked
Beside the lake, and listened to it sob,
As if the heart-aches of all human hearts
Were hidden in it, and his strong soul shook
With a great storm of passion.   "Help me," he
 prayed,
"O God, to do the thing I ought.   I hate
The social forms which made her rich, me poor,
With neither praise nor blame to her or me;
That make the inward good the outward wrong;
That rob earth of its glory and its grace,
And make a man's life war with manfulness;
But since these things are, help me, God, to be

Heroic, strong and noble." So he prayed.
The smiling August moon rose from the lake,
And clambered into heaven among the stars,
Leaving a silver trail across the waves
He felt the shadow of an unseen woe
Slanting across the future years, until
It sloped to meet his footsteps. So he prayed,
Until he felt his heart and purpose strong—
Felt through his inmost being all the strength
The triumph of self over self can give.

So when they sat within the marble gaze
Of Schiller's statue gleaming through the trees
Clasping some tender poem in its hand,
While snowy moonlight drifted through the shade,
Said Walter, "Edith, I have done you wrong;
I will not wrong you further." Edith turned,
A mingled shade and splendor on her face,
As comes a cloud at morning from the east,
Trailing the sunrise: "If you love me not,
Then have you spoken wisely."
                                        "Nay," he said,
"Say not, if I love not, but, if I love
So much that I would rather die than bring
A weight of care and trouble on your life.
I give my heart a willing sacrifice,
And in that sacrifice my heart is strong,
To spare you grief and trouble."
                                    "Listen," she said,
"You give your heart a willing sacrifice
To spare me grief and trouble, and you make

A life-long anguish for us both; I give
A little ease I love not over much,
And in the sacrifice my heart is strong,
To make you joy, and both of us are blest.
Which sacrifice is nobler—yours or mine?"
Her sweet, firm voice and gentle strength of will
Shook his strong soul, and in her tender smile
He felt his purpose vanish, like a drift
Of foolish snow beneath an April sun.
Stoop through the heavens, thou blushing August moon,
And lay thy full, red cheek against the dark!
Open unto their uttermost, ye stars,
Your bright, unwearying eyelids! It is light—
More light we want on earth. Then Walter bowed
His head upon his breast, and clasped her hands:
"Choose, Edith, for us both—I cannot choose."
She answered softly, "Walter, I have chosen!"

Night in the city, and its ponderous heart
Begins to beat low with the jar and clash
Of change and exchange half-subsiding. Lo,
There souls are dying—souls are being born.
Hark!—some are praying, and not far away
The sound of wassail, and the gambler's oath
Who loses, and his chuckle who wins. Hark!—
The moan of anguish, like the wandering wind
Amid the naked branches, and, dear God,
The very babes have curses on their lips,
Who know not what a curse means. Hark!—the sound

Of gospel singing, and not far away
The babble of the drunkard, and, lo! there
A little twelve-year girl is taken up drunk
From off the stones, and laid in the patrol.
O God, how can your angels sing in heaven,
With sights and sounds like these on one pale star?
Yonder the thief prepares his midnight tools,
The murderer like a serpent stealthily seeks
An ambush, where he coils and waits his prey.
Lo, there a three-months' bride, with streaming tears,
Showers her passionate kisses on cold lips
That but an hour since answered kiss with kiss.
Some word of hope strikes bell-like deep and sweet,
With multiple echoes. Listen!—do you hear
The music of a lover's first kiss? Hush!—
The sobbing of a lonely heart that breaks,
Like a wild wave upon a desolate shore,
Thrice lonely in a city full of hearts.
Across the rainbow fringes of the light,
The mirthful murmur of some social joust
Is heard not far away, and from the lake
The pale fog-angel comes and spreads his wings,
Smoke tinged, above the city; over all
The passionless stars, in bright, eternal hush,
Unsleeping ever, almost seem to sleep.

This night came Edith in her fleecy robe,
And nestled like a lamb between his knees,
Who laid a hand upon her shining head,
And waited for her word. She gently said:

"My father, can it be that you forget
How you once wed, against the wish and will
Of all your kindred, a poor simple girl,
Who made three years of life so sweet to you,
You could not love another? Do you hold
My love more cheaply? Father, I have chosen."
She thought his fond caressing touch a sign
Of melting, but 'twas only as the brook,
After the first frost, feels the morning sun,
And thaws a little, but congeals again
Into a twofold winter iciness,
After it feels the second night of frost.
The force of will that in his youth was strength,
The winter in his blood made obstinacy.
So men do sometimes nurse some foolish wish
And give the dearest thing they hold in life
Rather than calmly yield it to events.
The hand slipped downward from the shining head,
And Robert Earle arose, and thrice he strode
Across the room and thrice again, then turned,
And motioned her to leave him: "Go!" he said,
"Henceforth I am alone and childless. Go!"
She gave a sharp cry like a wounded thing,
And sprang into his arms, and clasped his neck:
"Edith, your rose! My father, say it not!"
He tore away the tender arms that clung
Like ivy tendrils to his bosom: "Go,
And come not back again, except,—" he smiled
A scornful, bitter smile that burned itself
Into her bosom, where it ached and throbbed
Heart-like unto her dying day—"except

You or your children hunger, or are cold,
Or shelterless, then come to me again,
And I will give you shelter, bread and clothes."
She turned, and like a wounded bird that tries
After the hunter's shot to fly again
But flutters helplessly along the grass,
She crept away to Walter, where he stood,
Leaning against a pillar of the porch.
She slipped her hand in his, and whispered, "Come!"
She looked so white and wounded that he caught
Both fluttering hands, and held her gently back:
"Choose yet again," he said, and gravely bent
And kissed her with a long and passionate kiss.
The spirit of a sweet smile, timorous, bright,
Uncertain if it dare to light at all,
Hovered about her young lips' tempting red:
"It is not yet too late—choose once again!"
And Edith answered, "Walter, I have chosen."

PART II

LIFE

So Edith Earle and Walter Gray were wed,
And made their nest up in a pleasant flat,
Upon a quiet street, and merrily chirruped
And sang like birds about its furnishing.
Then Edith set herself to learn new arts,
Turning her pretty hands to homely tasks,
Laughing about her blunders and mishaps,

Rehearsing them to Walter with such art
And graceful humor that he also laughed,
Until the tears would come. And many a night
They walked and talked together, while they heard
The restless waters moaning to the shore
Their sad, mysterious longings, that awake
Emotions that have lain too deep for thought,
As thought will often lie too deep for words.
They watched the people thronging to and fro
Beneath the lamplight—lovers hand in hand,
Grave men and women weary and worn with toil,
And children bubbling over with young life;
All waiting for the wave-washed winds that come
Whispering shoreward, shaking their cool wings.
And so they walked and talked and read and dreamed,
All in a rosy mist of life and love;
And so the summer and the autumn went
And Edith never spoke of that deep wound,
Too deep for time's slow healing.

       Christmas came,
The glad, white Christmas. "Our first Christmas-
 time,"
He whispered as he clasped her, and she smiled.
But Walter thought the smile was mixed with shade,
Like sunlight with the shadows of the leaves.
He looked at her so keenly that she dropped
Her lashes low to hide the blinding tears,
Saying, "We are so happy, but you know
The brightest day will have a little cloud,
And there's a mournful thought creeps to my heart—
My father sits alone and sad to-night."

She lifted up her eyes and saw his face
Was grave and troubled, and she blamed herself
For having spoken of it. Every day
She watched and waited for the tender word:
"Edith, my rose, my darling, come to me!"—
The word that never came. Oh, dull, slow pain
Of watching for a good that does not come,
And which the watcher has no power to speed!
Still Edith's heart beat lightly, for she hoped,
And life and love were young and strange and sweet.
So was it that almost before she knew
That they had come, the weeks and months flashed by,
Like shining sheets of water and green groves
And banks of flowers, seen from a flying train.
Edith was never used to hoard and count
The pennies, and; although she planned and saved
And calculated wisely, yet she found,
As household cares increased, expenditures
Exceeded income, and with all her thrift,
She could not make the two perverse ends meet.
She spoke no word to Walter, but she sold
The jewels from her casket one by one,
Telling herself she should not wear them more,
And meantime she would find a better way.
A shadow sometimes crept across her brow,
A look of anxious trouble in her eyes,
But Walter only saw the perfect smile.

It happened once upon a holiday
That Walter sat with Edith in the house,
When many flags were flying in the sun,

Orchestral music throbbing through the streets,
And all the city in its gay attire,
For Walter took his holidays for rest.
He held a book, and thinking that he read,
She propped her elbow on her knee, and leaned
Her chin upon her hand, and gravely gazed
Upon the busy street, but nothing saw
Of all the life and tumult that were there.
She saw before and after, and there came
A look of anxious trouble in her eyes.
And Walter, with his book before his face,
Seeming to read, but looking keenly at her
Over the top, observed the troubled gaze,
The sudden shadow cross the sunny brow,
As swift and noiseless as a flying world
Across the golden forehead of the sun.
He felt a sudden anguish in his breast,
As if his heart had beat against a thorn.
"Does she pine for the old life with its ease,
Its pleasure and its plenty? Does she hide
A stinging, live regret within her heart
Forever, like a wasp within a rose?"
He leaned a little forward, speaking low:
"Edith, my darling, could you choose again
To-day, would you so choose? I thought I saw
A shadow of regret upon your brow."
She turned to meet his hungry questioning gaze
Then bent to brush away a teasing fly
That troubled little Robert's rosy dream,
Who lay upon his pillow flushed and fair,
With dewy breath of sleep from unseen flowers,

And cool, white fountains sparkling in green glades.
She laid a hand upon his rosy palm,
Flung out upon the pillow like a flower,
Then turned again to Walter, speaking low:
"Oh! life has many sweet relationships,
The tender ties that hold the heart to earth
Through which its pulses run but to return
Enriched upon the heart—the sweet upflow
From child to parent, like the gentle dew
Sent down from heaven returned to heaven again;
The passionate out-gush from friend to friend,
Lover to lover, wedded heart to heart,
Brother to brother, like the pure exchange
Of limpid lakes, through secret hidden springs;
The pure down-flow from parent unto child,
Divinely tender, sweet, mysterious;
And more than these; but, wanting one of these,
The heart-aches for a thing missed out of life.
Oh! do not blame me, Walter, if I miss
My father's gentle hand upon my head,
Where oft it lay so fondly."
       After that
There came a little song-bird to the nest,
The sweetest, gladdest thing that ever ruled,
The queen and rosy despot of a home.
And Walter's heart was full as a full cup,
With the sweet wine of gladness, as he watched
The baby with her mother's eyes and hair,
The little leaping, laughing, loving thing,
Growing from day to day. And when, at last,
They walked abroad at eve, the little ones

Running before them hand in hand a way,
Now pausing to await their graver steps,
Or question them about some curious thing;
Or Walter lifted one, and Edith one,
With rosy mouths and blue eyes wonder wide,
To gaze upon the jarring, roaring wheels
Of some great engine panting at its task,
Like a fierce captive giant, and they strove
To smooth and tame some mighty idea down
To suit the grasping of the baby brain,
Then Walter's heart was full as a full cup.
So was it that his life flashed into song,
Burst into sunlight, like a river that runs
A long time through a dark, deep gorge, then breaks
Out on a ledge, leaps down a rock, and sweeps
Into a sunlit valley, where it glides,
Untroubled as a child's first thought of God.
The man was gayer than the boy had been;
'Tis marvelous how much we change with change.

But Edith's life grew graver, for to her
Was more of loss as well as more of gain.
How could he understand what she had missed?
The gay, bright world she came from—like a bird
From golden tropics with their cloudless skies,
The deathless bloom of flowers, and the sound
Of music that could make the angels weep,
The social life and splendor, and the light
Of friendly faces, waiting for her smile
To breathe their homage, and, the best of all,
The tender touch upon her shining hair

Of one dear hand, the fond light of one smile;—
Came, like a rare bird shedding its bright hues,
Daring the northern bleakness, blast and frore,
And wearing sober plumes to match its mate.
She sometimes felt a hunger for these things,
And chafed a little at the long, dull days'
Unyielding bonds of duty—she, whose will
Was never thwarted, who had never felt,
Through childhood's happy May or girlhood's June,
The thorn-thrust of a sharp, unyielding no;
And Walter sometimes vexed her with his eyes,
Searching her through and through to find some spark
Of smoldering regret or discontent.
Less noble natures had grown irritable,
But Edith bravely trod the secret thorns,
And ever told herself his gravest fault
Was loving her too fondly; and each day
She battled with herself heroically.
And Walter only saw the perfect smile,
And asked no other splendor in his life,
No music but the laughter of his babes,
That kept his young heart full as a full cup,
So full it needed but a little jar
To spill a portion of the joyous wine.

Once in the morning paper, Walter came
Upon the name of Lucius Coventry.
He read the name aloud, and after it
The brilliant marriage notice, and then cast
A sidelong, searching glance at Edith. She

On either shoulder laid a loving hand,
And looked down with a mirthful, quivering smile;
A smile that, like a sunbeam on her lips,
A sunbeam falling between tremulous leaves,
Quivering like golden water on the floor,
Danced back and forward playfully,—a smile
That made him blush with conscious foolishness,
And in confusion draw the bright face down
For tender kissing, and read hastily on.

Upon a shining morn when Walter romped
With little Elsa ere he went from home,
He tossed her lightly like a rose, then caught
Her falling flushed into his hands,
Then tossed her high in air again, and cried,
"Elsa, my rose!" and caught her to his breast.
Then how the tiny maiden leaped and laughed,
As if she heard a sweet, familiar sound,
A name the angels whispered in her ears,
Just as they kissed her at the brink of earth.
But Edith whitened with a sudden pain,
As when a sudden storm is on the lake,
And quick as thought she crossed to Walter's side,
Before the after, wiser thought had come,
And laid rebuking hands upon his lips:—
"Not that name, Walter, do not call her that!"
He dropped the child, who, feeling herself wronged
At being so rudely treated, wailed with grief.
He looked in Edith's face, as one who dreams,
Or half awake still fancies that he dreams,
And heard a smothered sob in the white throat.

He passed into the street, and seemed to see
All things like flitting shadows through a mist.
Men jostled him; a cabman, reining back.
Cursed his slow steps. He heard the rush and roar,
Far-off, like distant breakers on a beach.
And all day long he heard that smothered sob
Which made him start and blunder at his work.
Again the shadow of an unseen woe
Slanted across the future years and sloped
To meet his shuddering footsteps, and he shrank.

At evening Edith met him with her smile,
Unfailing as the sunset. She observed
His unaccustomed silence, questioned him,
If he were troubled, very tired or ill.
He only pressed his hand against his brow,
And Edith, thinking that his head ached, stroked
His forehead with her cool, soft finger tips.
She early hushed the children at their play,
Sent Robert to his pictures, and took up
The little prattling Elsa on her knees,
And hummed to her a drowsy, silvery tune,
Until the golden head reluctantly
Drooped on the mother's bosom like a flower.

Another morning Walter went from home
To hear through all the day that smothered sob
Which made him start and blunder at his work.

At evening Edith met him clad in white,
And smiling like the sunset. She observed

His silence, but refrained from questioning.
She early hushed the children at their play,
And with the little Elsa on her arm,
Flushed with the mystic beauty of deep sleep,
Rocked gently to and fro, and softly sang.
She lifted up her eyes—she knew not why,
Except that something drew her, and observed
That Walter's eyes were looking keenly at her.
"Walter, what vexes you?" she gently said.
"Oh! silence may be best when all is well,
When thoughts outrun the slowlier-moving words
To meet and kiss, and hearts keep perfect time,
But wrong makes wrong of silence, when a word
Might, like a sunbeam, melt the ice which else
Would grow too thick for warm hearts to beat
  through;
And he is no true lover or true friend,
Who will not bravely speak the fault that flaws.
'Tis noble to forgive—'tis nobler still
To ask to be forgiven; and this I know,
That even if frankness should be harshly met,
'Twere better pride should bear a little wound
Than risk the life-long aching of two hearts."
Walter arose, still looking keenly at her,
And bent above her, whitening as he spoke:
"Edith, I have been watching you of late,
And, oh! it breaks my heart to see you grieve
For that of which I robbed you. It was this—
The fear of this that haunted all my dreams
Like a dark spectre ere I called you mine."
A flame of anger flashed in Edith's heart,

One said once, "Love is blind," and thereby erred;
With eagle eyes she faces the soul's blaze,
Sees finest flaws where she craves perfectness,
But, being so patient, seemeth not to see.
Then Edith dropped her face upon her hands,
And battled with herself heroically,
Repeating to herself, "His gravest fault
Is loving me too well. Help me," she prayed,
"O God, to do the thing I ought, to be
Patient and true and gentle." Walter stood
Looking upon her, knowing not she prayed.
She lifted up her face bathed in a smile
That lit her like an angel: "Walter, listen!—
'Tis vain to watch; what life is sorrowless?
Our very joys make shadows, as the birds
And fruits and flowers that make earth beautiful,
All cast a little shadow in the sun.
The joy you brought me took some joy away.
Forgive me, Walter, for if I could choose
Again to-day, 'twould be as I have chosen.
Be patient with me, Walter, when I miss
The tender face, whose never-clouded smile
Made rosy all the morning of my life."
He drew her toward him, till her shining head
Lay trembling like a meteor on his breast:
"Edith, forgive the shadow of distrust;
'Tis love's intensity makes its own clouds.
Forgive me, darling, that I hurt you so."
Then Edith looked up, smiling in his eyes,
Saying, "Love's rapier, like Achilles' spear,
Has ever power to heal the wounds it makes."

So Walter's heart beat joyously again,
And swiftly flew the days like happy birds.
O happy years, O happy, hurrying years,
Why is it ye are mad with haste? Behold
The lagging of the sorrowful, slow years.

One winter night, when all the air was full
Of the faint, fairy music of the snow,
Soft, rustling wings of gently jostling flakes,
Walter and Edith sat and read by turns,
And now the "Romance of the Swan's Nest" read,
While Robert sat near by, with book and slate,
And little Elsa, perched upon the arm
Of a great rocker, swaying to and fro,
Sat singing like a linnet on a limb,
The music swelling in her tiny throat,
And over all the glowing grate-fire threw
Its rosy warmth and color. Walter read
Just as the song began. His father's heart
Swelling with pride, he paused a while to listen,
Then bent toward Edith, whispering cautiously,
Lest he should fright the warbler from her song,
Asking if she had marked the wondrous voice,
And Edith smiled and nodded. When at last
The carol was quite finished, Walter sprang,
And caught the little songster in his arms,
And tossed her high, and caught her in his hands,
Waving her hands and feet in mad delight,
And tossed her high again, and cried, "My bird!
Now the old tyrant hunter has you fast."
And ever after called the child his bird.

Now Edith's costly jewels were all sold
From out the casket where they erst had lain,
Twinkling like stars within a midnight sky,
Single and double stars and clusters rare;
And still, although she worked and planned and saved,
She could not make the two perverse ends meet.
"I will not speak to Walter," Edith said,
"Because a girl less delicately bred
Had been a better wife to Walter—yes,
Had made our modest income easily
Supply the household needs, and educate
And clothe the little ones; no, I must find
Some work to do, the while they are at school,
And Walter need not know." But what and how,
Were ever restless questions in her brain.

There came what in this clouded hour appeared
A sunbeam, but which darkened afterward.
So seems each blessing sometimes half a curse,
Each angel shape that gleams athwart the gloom,
Constrained to dip its wings in some dark pool.
Martha, the good nurse, who had fondly watched
Her infant slumbers, loved her as her own,
Came to her on a late autumnal day.
"My heart was sick to see my pretty child,"
She cried, the strong arms round the slender neck,
Bending it forward like a lily stalk,
Almost to breaking. "Is my sweet child well?
And is my white dove happy with her mate?
You ought to hear how the fine people talk."

"What say the people, Martha?" Edith asked.
"They say you were a silly, senseless girl
To slight a man like Lucius Coventry,
Who is, they say, a kind of natural king,
And take up with a clown like Walter Gray;
And now, no doubt, you're miserable enough."
Then Edith crimsoned from her slender throat
Up to the golden edges of her hair.
"Tell them," she said, "that I am happy; say,
I'd not change kings with any queen on earth.
What of my father? Tell me, is he well,
And does he ever seem to miss his rose?"
"Miss you, dear heart?—I've never seen him smile
Ever so faintly since the night you went.
'Twould make you weep to see him wandering
From room to room, so white and shadow-like.
The hand that lifts the goblet to his lips
Trembles so pitifully! Miss you?—he keeps
Your room just as it was the night you went.
Sometimes he bids us air and dust it, then
He goes to see that all things are replaced—
The white dress lightly thrown across the chair,
The handkerchief you dropped upon the floor,
The Bible open, with the passage marked
Where Ruth clings to Naomi with sweet words.
I've heard him pacing up and down your room
At midnight, and one night I heard him groan."
Like April sky was Edith's streaming face,
Half shining, half in shower, glad to be missed,
But sad to think of him so sorrowful.
Said Martha, cuddling up the little one,

"If he could only see the cherub here,
As like her mother as I ever saw
A perfect rosebud like a perfect rose,
His heart would melt—I'm very sure of that.'
Then Martha's talk went wandering through events,
Things done, things rumored done, unspoken words
That should be spoken, spoken ones best unsaid,
Like wind through tangled grasses, till at last,
The swift autumnal twilight scared away
The yellow sunbeams sleeping on the floor.
When she arose to take her final leave,
She took the delicate face 'twixt her large hands,
And held it long, and kissed it many times—
Now grown more lily-like than like a rose:
"You are quite happy then, my pretty child?"
"Quite happy, only—" and the sweet voice hung
Upon that word as caught upon a thorn.
O human heart, that bitter only hides
In the all-perfectness of every joy.
"Ah! only what?" Then Edith simply told
How, never being used to count the cost,
And save the pennies, she could scarcely make
Their modest income meet their household needs,
And now the little ones were sent to school,
The days were long and lonely, and she thought
'Twere better could she find some work to do
To help a little, and fill up the hours;
Could Martha think of something? Martha took
The delicate hands between her ample palms,
And stroked and kissed and patted them and wept,
As if to coax from them some happy thought:

"To think these pretty hands must toil for bread,
And plenty wasted in your father's house!—
But I will set my little wit to work,
And try to think of something they can do."
Then she remembered how those fingers flashed
Over the gleaming keys, and under them,
The sound of winds and rippling rivulets,
The song of birds, the crash of waterfalls
And tender, tearful sounds that stir the heart
With mystical, sweet sorrow, as of things
Known in another life, and now forgot,
Except in these faint, waking moments. Then
She queried, why not write to some old friends,
The best and kindest, frankly ask of them
To let her teach their children? Edith smiled:
"I thank you, Martha, I will think of it."
And she did think of it for nights and days,
And tried to tell herself if it were wise.

One day she leaned against the window sill,
Turning the problem over in her brain,
When a tall liveried coachman on his seat,
By his familiar motions caught her glance.
Within a man sat waiting. Edith's heart
Beat hard against her bosom, like a hand
With close-shut fingers upon prison bars.
Then Martha's words came echoing in her ears,
"If he could only see the cherub here,
His heart would melt—I'm very sure of that."
She called the little Elsa from her play:
"Come, birdie, take these pennies here, and run

Where yonder stands the old banana man
Upon the corner; he is old and lame,
And all day long has had but little trade;
His fruit will surely spoil. Now run away
And see how quickly you can come again.
Be careful, darling, when you cross the street,
And do not fall upon the slippery stones,
Or get before the horses." Like a bird,
Wing-swift, away the little maiden flew,
And Edith watched the fairy figure dart
Amid the jostling throng, the little feet
Twinkling across the stones, the yellow curls
Dancing behind her in the autumn wind.
She drives her little bargain, and receives,
Because of rosy cheeks and flying curls,
A whole banana over purchase price.
Now, swift returning, come the flying feet;
A second time they pass the carriage door;
Will he not see her? Edith's heart beats loud,
Beat tripping beat, they seem to come so fast.
What stays the flying feet? Has some one called?
A white head from the carriage leans and looks.
The old man, stepping to the pavement, takes
The little wondering maiden in his arms.
One hand is laid upon the shining hair,
And Edith bows her head, and almost thinks
'Tis on her head that gentle hand is laid.
He kisses her on either glowing cheek,
Then fumbles in his pocket till he finds
Pencil and paper, writes some hurried words,
And slips the paper in the dimpled hand.

A blinding mist comes over Edith's eyes;
She hears the fairy tread upon the stairs;
It comes at last, the happy word has come:
"Edith, my rose, my darling, come to me!"
She holds the crumpled paper to her lips,
Then opens it with trembling hands and reads:
"Give me the child; the child is not to blame,
And I will give her such a bringing up,
As will be worthy her, and worthy me.
Give me the child." And then the trembling name.
Then Edith dropped her face upon her hands,
And in her heart the flame of hope died down.
Between her fingers ran the swift, bright tears,
One after other fast and faster fell,
Until it seemed there were no more to weep,
As when, once having broken a string of pearls,
Each after each slips, leaving a pearlless string.
"My father, O my father, is it well
To tear your rose out of your bosom so?"

Edith arose, and resolutely turned
Her face upon the future, and her back
On all the hopeless sorrows of the past;
And then she wrote, in frank and courteous way,
Some letters to the friends of other days,
The best and kindest, saying modestly,
They would recall how, in her girlhood days,
She loved the art of music best of all;
And now the the little ones were sent to school,
The days were long and lonely, and she thought
To fill the hours with pleasant work, and so

Increase their modest income; would they let
Her teach their children—she would strive to please.
A prompt and kindly answer came from each.
Said Edith with her blue eyes full of tears—
"The world is not so cruel after all.
Oh! many a heart is full of gentleness,
Sweet, copious springs of kindness, if we will
But bend a little to receive it." So,
Lightlier Edith's heart beat spite its wound,
And cheerily she daily worked and planned,
And saved a little, saying to herself,
When Walter's brief vacation came again,
Beside some still, blue lake or running stream,
Where there is heard no more distracting life
Than folding and unfolding water lilies,
Singing of birds, dew-drinking of the flowers,
Sighing of trees and grasses, and the stir
Of sweet, unsullied air, the livelong day,
Far off from all the city's dust and din,—
There they would pass their second honeymoon.
Walter would look at her in mild surprise,
And wonder how she saved it. She would smile
Into his eyes, and answer playfully,
"Would any untaught maiden bred to toil,
Know better how to scrimp and save than she?"
And then she thought how Walter's eyes would shine
With unshed tears, and how his sweet, firm lips
Would tremble with unspoken words of love.
The unsought bliss of which we never dream,
Comes to us with a fuller wave of joy,
Because the rosy cup drained suddenly

No bitter lees of disappointment has.
But, oh, the pictured rapture of a dream,
O'er which the heart bends, flushed with ecstasy,
Supplying here and there a tender shade
Or happy gleam of color! Never doubt
But that some cruel chance, with mocking hand,
Will draw a blighting brush across your work
Ere it has passed into reality.

One of the happiest of happy-days,
Just as the purple jags of twilight fit
Into the golden edges of the day,
Walter and Edith, in the Sabbath calm,
Gazed at the sweet, veiled future reverently,
That stood like Isis, robed in mystery,
When, like a wild bird fluttering through the door,
A dainty little maiden flitted in:
She could not take her lessons for a week,
And teased to come and bring the word herself.
So saying, the pretty babbler wound her arms
About the neck of Edith, who, confused
And vexed to find her secret out, returned
The child's caress, but looked at Walter; he
Looked first at Edith, then upon the child,
Like one who has been wakened suddenly;
And when the innocent mischief-maker went,
He murmured, "Edith, is it then so bad?
Is it so hard to make our little reach
To all our needs? So often I have seen
The weary flush upon your cheek at night,
The drooping of your eyelids, and the lines

Of patient care about your sunny mouth."
Edith replied: "O Walter, be not vexed!
The days were long and lonely, and I thought
To fill the empty hours with pleasant work.
Perhaps we have enough for simple needs,
But is it well to keep our lives pent up
In such a narrow channel? Let me help
To widen out our pathway through the world."
Walter could make no answer, but her words
Went ringing bell-like on from thought to thought.
Edith was silent, knowing not his mind,
Fearing her words might jar upon his mood.

At morn he kissed her silently, and went
Down the long street, where darkly rolled the tide
Of roaring life, till at the open bridge,
It foamed and fretted, while the splendid boat
Swept like a stately swan toward the blue lake,
Churning the stagnant water to faint foam.
On plunged the tide again with deafening roar,
And Walter swept on with it. What was that?—
The man before him dropped a little pack
Of papers on the pavement. Walter stooped
Mechanically, and took it up to see
If there were aught of value, and he saw
A check was in the package, and made haste
To overtake the loser, but he swept
Around the corner, like a drifting leaf
Caught by a counter current, and sucked down
Into the raging vortices of life.
So Walter placed the check within his desk,

And there it lay for three days. On the third,
He chanced upon it; it had been forgotten.
"Only a thousand, but enough to make
My darling's pathway blossom for a while,
Whose delicate feet had trod on dewy flowers,
Had I not led her out on this bleak way."
It seemed as if a mist on Walter's brain
Lay like the fog, that, rising from the lake,
Rolled dark above the city that day, and made
The noontime as the night, and through the fog
He heard the words of Edith toll like bells.
The pen was in his fingers, where it hung,
Vibrating like the delicate beam of fate,
On which a floating feather or a breath,
Falling, tips suddenly toward good or ill.
He held it quivering, till a breath of pain
Jostled the springs of will; then Walter bent,
And with a few strokes signed forever away
His right to honor, peace and happiness.
Forging the payee's name upon the check,
He cashed it with the money of the house
And tossed it blindly in a secret drawer.
That night a gentle wind arose and swept
The dense fog from the city, and revealed
The passionless, pure stars, and Walter woke.
The gentle breath of sleep had blown away
The vapors from his brain; thought after thought
Flashed out of his unclouded consicousness—
What he had done, what might come of that deed.
An icy horror ran along his veins;
His heart seemed bursting with its frozen tears.

Then Edith, breathing softly, slipped her hand
In his, as by command of some sweet thought
Escaped the slumbering will, and Walter rose,
Put on his garments, left a little note
For Edith, saying he was called away.
He leaned above the dark lake from the pier,
And listened to it rub its shaggy sides
Against its prison bars with mournful moan,
Like a dumb, helpless creature, hurt and bound,
And felt a fascination in his blood
To leap and end his anguish. So he leaned
And looked, until his brain swam with the waves.
Even so a man looks in upon himself,
And thinks upon himself, until his brain
Grows giddy, and he seems a mere machine.
Listen—the footfall of a passer-by,
That lonely hour, and near that lonely spot!
He started, but what matter?—no one cares,
In a great city, what another does,
Except you touch on his self-interest. Oh!
Observe!—he is alive and quivering then,
As if you had touched with a cold steel point
Upon a naked nerve. For Edith's sake
He must live on; perchance he might escape
The consequences of that rash, blind act;
But if they fell upon him he must live
To tell her that he did it for love's sake.
He thought how her old friends would wag their
    heads,
Smiling the devil's smile of cool sarcasm;
Of the grim triumph in her father's heart,

And then of Edith battling on alone;
Of all her shame and grief and loneliness;
Then of his children with their sullied names.
So many pale forms of that one grief paced
Through the dim chambers of his brain, for so
The knife of agony has many blades:
Grief never cutteth with a single edge.
The unseen woe, whose shadow went before,
Had fallen upon him, and he wrestled there
In anguish, till the stars were all dissolved
Into the rosy dawn, like pearls in wine.
For many days he thought he slept too sound,
So sound his head ached with a weary dream
Of prison walls, and courts, and unjust men,
Rushing his trial through with cruel haste,
Unto the bitter sentence—ten blank years
Of prison life, dead, miserable years.

He fancied he slept still, when Edith knelt
And laid her shining head against his breast:
"Speak to me, Walter! Walter, speak to me!
Walter, I cannot live unless you speak!"
Then Walter looked, and knew that it was day.
He saw the glow and glory of the west,
As the sad sunshine slipped along the world,
Wooing the darkness; for, to eyes that weep,
The sunshine seemeth sadder than the night.
"Edith," he murmured incoherently,
"Is it worth while to try to live again,
And come to you again with prison taint
Upon my lips, to kiss you and the babes?"

"O Walter, try to live, and let our love,
Through years of parting grow more ripe and sweet,
And I will teach the little ones to watch
Your coming, talking much of you to keep
Your memory unfaded in their hearts;
And, Walter, I will strive to have them grow
Noble and beautiful to welcome you."
"You do not scorn me then, my darling?"
                                        "Scorn?
Walter, you did it just for love of me.
Now if a pure soul do a righteous thing
For love's sake, that being easy, who shall say,
That if a noble nature wound itself,
Doing a thing ignoble for love's sake,
That being so hard, this love is less divine?"
He leaned his noble brow on the bright head,
And shuddered with a mighty storm of grief,
Bathing her sweet face in his streaming tears,
That mingled with her own like blending showers.
The children, standing by, and seeing them weep,
Wept for the grief they could not understand,
Except as if a cloud had crossed the sun,
And flung a sudden shadow over them,
And hid the smile upon the lips of love.
A kindly officer with tear-wet eyes
Took up the little Elsa in his arms,
And held a colored picture to her view,
Whereat a ripple of childish laughter drove
Away the cloud, and checked the falling tears,
As a light wind might chase a summer shower;
But little Robert's face was very grave.

"My Edith," Walter murmured, "had you known,
On that last night of choice, what you now know,
Would you have chosen then as you did choose?
But say it once again, and I will live
After these ten long, lifeless years in tomb.
Thank God, love is immortal!" Edith rose,
Upon her girlish face, around which clung
Her soft hair like a golden evening cloud,
The light of an ineffable love which glowed
Like the reflected gleam of angel wings
From some far height of heaven. "Walter," she said,
"If I had looked, on that last night of choice,
Down the long, winding way of life which led
From that bright *then*, even to this sad *now*,
And seen the thorns awaiting for my feet,
Even this height of anguish at the end,
Crowned with the snows of unwept, frozen tears,
I should have chosen then as I did choose."

PART III

DEATH

So Edith sold her pretty furniture,
And took a room upon a noisy street,
Where all day long hoarse, inarticulate cries
Of the street venders, and the beat of hoofs,
The rumble of heavy carts, and the shrill scream
Of fretful mothers for their truant brood,
The wrangling of rude children, and the broils

Of miserably mismated men and women,
The din of barter, the discordant shriek
Of jangling whistles, and the poison breath
Of the green river, crawling like a snake
Under the bending bridges, and the fog,
Mixed with the breath of factories that keeps
The golden sunlight tarnished, and beneath,
The black, unresting stream of human life,
Wearied the senses from the dawn till night.
Then out the tired people swarmed like flies,
And crawled upon the pavements and the steps,
And clung about the windows and the doors,
And so they gossiped, laughed and quarreled and
    sang.
But now the autumn wind, with cutting edge,
Early drove in the people, and maintained
A kind of nightly silence in the street.

Edith toiled bravely on from day to day,
With breaking heart, but with a steadfast will.
It is so hard to spin life's golden threads
With steady hand, and no one by to say,
"How fares thy work?" or, "Love, it is well done."
But Edith kept the little ones in school
And comfortably clothed and fed, and so
The glad, white Christmas came and went, and
    seemed
No Christmas without Walter.
                                  When again
The sun moved north with summer in his arms,
The little Elsa drooped like some frail flower.

A languor came upon her, and all day
She sat beside the window, her blue eyes
Turned listlessly upon the busy street.
Then Edith rose at sunrise every day,
And took the little ones to breathe the air,
That from the lake, which in the morning sun,
Like waves of liquid silver darkly gleamed,
Came hastening shoreward, spray-washed, sweet
 and clean.
The children played together in the sands,
Or watched the boatmen sponging out their boats,
Or the white sails upon the distant sky,
Or troops of men and boys that cityward
Went wending, carrying long strings of fish;
Or laughed with glee, as one retreating wave,
And one that hurried shoreward, winged with foam,
Met and leaped up together in the sun,
And grappled, white with anger, and rolled over,
Struggling, dissolving in each other's arms.
And sometimes, when the lake was wild and white,
The mad waves leaped upon the gray sea-wall,
Like wild, caged creatures, and fell back again,
Or, dashing over, chased with flying foam,
The shouting children, who had ventured near.
But often, when the lake was blue and still,
Save for light ripples made by gentle winds,
They gathered stones, and tossed them in to see
How soon the silver dint was smoothed away.
But Edith sat apart, and sadly smiled,
Or spoke some gentle word of kindly cheer
To women, who had brought their sickly babes

. To drink the sweet air, ere the risen sun
Had sapped its strength and sweetness. Oft she took
The puny little creatures in her arms,
To rest the tired mothers, while she asked,
With sweet, compassionate looks, inviting trust,
How life went with them. "Hard enough!" said one.
Her husband had a head for something great,
Handled machines as children play with toys,
But a long, wasting fever laid him low,
Just when the little home was almost theirs.
And what with payments due and doctor's bills,
And keeping of the family, all was gone;
The mortgage was foreclosed, and all was gone.
"How many children?"
"Eight, too young to work,
And one a cripple, one this sickly babe."
Another said her husband lost his place
To make room for a foreman's favorite.
He was disheartened, and had taken to drink,
And who was there to feed six hungry mouths?
And since the little one was cutting teeth,
And fretting with the fever day and night,
How could she leave it now and go away
From home to labor? Edith's gentle heart
Ached for the great world's sorrow, and her breast
Swelled with a holy anger, as she raised
Her eyes, and saw within the morning sun
The gleam of princely mansions, and she cried,
"It is unjust, dear God, it is unjust,
That a few men should idly waste enough
To lift up multitudes; that hearts should break,

And souls go down to hell, all for the want
Of such a little of their magic gold
As would not cause the lady slumbering there
Behind her silken curtain, to deprive
Her poodle of a single lap of cream.
O God, the earth is bright and beautiful,
So lovely that we laugh with pain-warped lips,
And stored with ample riches for us all;
Why then are not men happier?"
                              "Aye, unjust!"
The woman said, "but tell it not to God!
What does he care for all our toil and pain?
Would I so smite my sweet child lying there,
And mix his golden curls with dust and tears,
Then hear him wailing, 'Mother, it is I,
Here by thy will not mine; then give to me
Enough to live without such agony!'
But God will hear us weeping unto death,
Praying till we lack breath, but will not check
One cloud in heaven, or speed one beam to earth,
For all our prayers, and weeping. It is strange
We get our air and sunshine without tax.
We'll take our sunlight bottled by and by,
And buy air in pound boxes."
                              In those days
The little Elsa brightened for a while,
But drooped again, and would not leave the house.
She sat beside the window, her blue eyes
Turned languidly upon the busy street.
She watched the children flitting to and fro,
With foaming pitchers of vile-smelling beer.

She liked to have the organ-grinder come
And sit upon the curb across the street,
And grind out his monotonous melodies;
Or, better still, the three Italian boys,
Who played upon the harp and violins
Some tender, plaintive melodies which struck
A hidden chord of sadness. Once she saw
A ragged woman searching with a stick
Among the garbage for discarded food.
Her blue eyes filled with pitying tears; she cried,
 She has no dinner for her little ones;
I am not hungry, mother; give her mine."
And once she saw a woman carrying
A barrel filled with kindling, on her back.
She hid her face behind her little hands,
And wept aloud, and Edith, bending, asked,
"What grieves my darling?"
      "Oh! I only thought,"
She sobbed, "dear mother, what if that were you!"

One morning, when the sun rose fierce and red,
The tired child took up her mother's hand,
And laid it on her flushed cheek coaxingly,
And murmured, "Do not leave me!" Edith sent
A message to her patrons, telling them
She could not come until the child was well.
And so, for many days she sat and watched
The wasting fever burn the little life
Low in its fragile socket, till at last
Only a faint spark flickered. All that day,
The cruel, yellow sun beat through the blinds;

And Edith hung in anguish o'er the child,
Bathing the burning lips and fevered brow,
And stroking back the tangled yellow curls,
Marking the wandering gaze of the blue eyes,
Speaking fond words, and praying in her heart.
While Robert hovered round his sister's couch,
And kissed the little burning hands, and asked
A thousand times, "Is sister better now?"
All day the little one tossed restlessly,
Moaning upon her pillow. When the eve
Closed in with clouds and thunder, Robert stood
And watched the bounding raindrops on the sill,
His young heart bathed with prayer like flower
  with dew,
Until the lamps were lighted in the street,
Then lay beside the little one to watch,
But, child-like, fell into a dreamless sleep.
And then, as if the shadow of sleep's soft wing
That brooded him, had touched the little one,
A light and troubled slumber fell on her.
Then Edith, falling prone, lay motionless,
As one that hath no strength to weep or moan,
Her delicate cheek pressed hard against the floor.
Out slipped the fastenings from her gleaming hair,
That rippled like a golden rivulet down,
And lay in shining waves along the floor.
Out burst the full moon like a lily in bloom,
Through clouds blown leaf-like open either side.
Then Edith cried a strong and bitter cry:
"Walter, O Walter, Walter!" and again —
"My father, O my father!" and then hushed

That sharp-edged cry upon her lips, for fear
That it might cut the silken cords of sleep,
Which bound the little sufferer a while.
Then all was midnight silence, save outside,
The boisterous laughter of a merry crowd
Of homeward-straggling revelers, and again—
A solitary whistler in the street,
The bellowing of a great boat at the bridge,
Or the fierce, petulant screaming of a tug,
And not far off the cry of a sick child.
Edith stretched forth her hands and softly prayed,
"Take me, O God, take me, but spare the child!"
The memory of a scornful, bitter smile
Was burning in her bosom like a flame,
Whose embers were the cruel words: "Except
You or your children hunger. . . . . ." and again—
"The child is not to blame; give me the child."
So saying to herself, "If I should die,
He would receive my children to his heart,
And love them as his own," she softly prayed,
"Take me, O God, take me, but spare the child."
Then, rising up, she saw a woman's form
Beside the couch, and started, pale with fear,
Thinking a phantom came to take the child.
But Martha said, "I heard the babe was ill,
And could not wait till morning." Edith fell
On Martha's bosom, weeping piteously.
And Martha folded her puissant arms
About the quivering form, and kissed her hair,
And soothed her like a sick and weary child.
Skilled in the art of nursing, Martha knew

The thing to do, and better still, the thing
Not to be done, and ere a week was gone,
A gentle moisture on the tender skin
Lay like the evening dew upon a rose
That has been drooping all a summer day.
Slowly the little life came fluttering back,
Like a reluctant bird, that, half escaped
Between the wires, is coaxed into its cage,
But not the joyous, bounding life of old.
The pale child leaned against her mother's knees,
And chirruped a few faint wood-notes plaintively,
Or oftener lay upon her mother's arm,
And listened to some pretty fairy tale;
And Edith had no heart to go away.
So in the chill autumnal days she searched,
And found some work that she could do at home.
The little Edith loved to sit and watch
Her mother's white hands flashing in and out
The rainbow-colored worsteds, as she wove
The green and crimson and the blue and gold
Into the little jackets, caps and skirts.

But medicines and coal and food and rent,
And clothing for the children, pressed her sore,
Till she was forced to find a cheaper room,
Up three long flights of stairs against the roof,
Which only had the strangled light and air,
That came through one small window opening out
Upon a gloomy passage, where the light,
Sallow and sickly, through a skylight fell.
And there, through many a dark and gloomy day,

She worked with aching eyes and throbbing brow,
Turning sometimes the gaslight on at noon,
And heard far off the roaring sea of life,
Like long, low thunder; scarcely marked at all
The languor of her limbs, the short, dry cough,
Or checked the flying fingers to abate
The sudden, cruel pain that pierced her chest.
And once a crimson rill burst from her lips,
And stained the purple jacket in her hands.

So the long, weary winter wore away,
And summer panted in the veins of earth.
Climbed little Elsa, on a day in June,
Up the steep, wooden stairs with dancing feet;
She had not moved so blithely for a year;
And Edith looked up smiling when she broke
All quivering like a sunbeam through the room.
Then breathlessly she told, with shining eyes,
How the rich lady in the great stone house
Around the corner, had two pretty dogs,
As white as snow, with noses black as jet,
With silver, tinkling bells around their necks,
With 'broidered crimson blankets over them,
That slept in baskets lined with gorgeous plush.
But after luncheon, when my lady slept,
The little darlings, at their merry play,
Disturbed her with their frolics; she would give
The little girl five cents an afternoon,
To watch them at their gambols, and restrain
Them when they grew too boisterous; could she go?
A crimson wave of anger overswept

The marble forehead; an indignant no
Trembled on Edith's lips; a second thought
Restrained it; no, it could not harm the child;
She would be better for more light and air,
And hours of frolic. "Yes, a little while,"
She said, "a while, till Robert's school is out."
And so my lady, who had gone abroad,
And bought the title nature had refused,
Slept tranquilly the golden afternoons,
While little Elsa tenderly restrained
Her boisterous pets, and sometimes wistfully
She gazed upon the dish of yellow cream
Their slender, scarlet tongues lapped daintily,
The tempting cakes they crumbed upon the floor.
Now when at four my lady went to drive,
On either side of her, complacently,
With canine gravity they sat and looked
Down on the little maiden, as she thought,
With lofty condescension, and, withal,
An arrogant, commiserating gaze.
"O mother," once she cried with tearful eyes,
"I wish I were a pretty little dog,
Just long enough to ride far, far away,
Where there are many birds and trees and flowers!"

The mother's heart grew bitter in her breast.
A morning came when Edith could not rise,
But struggled to her elbow, and fell back,
Fainting, upon her pillow. Days went on,
And still the busy fingers, white and limp,
Lay motionless upon the coverlid.

Veiled in the shadow of the night, she wept
Hot tears that burned her eyelids, murmuring,
"O Walter, I have tried to wait for you;
Were I a little stronger I could wait,
But I am tired, so tired, and sick at heart.
I'll wait for you in heaven—I am so tired!"
She wrote a letter in a tremulous hand,
And on the back, the name of Robert Earle,
And kissing it, as one might kiss a flower,
That some dear hand has touched, or soon will touch,
Placed it beneath her pillow, whispering,
"Not a reproachful word, my father, not one;
Your rose has no more thorns to hurt you with!
Not a regretful word, my father, not one;
Because my angels have been crowned with thorns,
They are not less my angels—I have chosen."
Spoke little Robert, bending over her,
"Dear mother, there is nothing left to eat."
Then Edith answered, wandering in her mind:
"How strange I should forget my little ones!
Wait, Robert, till I rest a little while,
Then I will rise and set you out some food."
Said Robert tenderly, his manly lips
All quivering with anguish, "I will go
And try to sell some papers; I will come
As quickly as I can, and bring some food."

The great sun, like a furnace of the gods,
Replenished with a hundred dead old worlds,
Blazed that day with a fierce and yellow glare,
Till, like a web of incandescent fire,

Woven above the city, its wires glowed,
And every shadow lay oasis-like,
Darkling within the desert of white light,
With gasping men and women overfull.
Horses and men sank in the reeking tide
Of human life, and every now and then,
A pale, white-sheeted form was borne away
To dismal morgue or hospital or home.
Like idle sails, the leaves hung listlessly.
The wretches used to sleeping in the sun,
At noontime, on the lake shore, crept away,
Seeking a shadow, for the blue lake slept,
Placid and pitiless, puffed its burning breath
Into the strangled city. With scorched cheeks,
And brows burned to their helmets, faithfully
The brave policemen faced the blasting sun,
Upon the blazing corners of the streets.
The sun went down in splendor, hemmed about
With sunset clouds upon each other heaped,
Like Pelion on Ossa. Peak on peak,
They piled in glory 'round the feet of night.
Then the clear stars, like mocking, tearless eyes,
Burned through the humid darkness and the lamps
Threw out their rainbow fringes.
                              "Paper, sir?
I cannot sell them, sir, and we have had
No supper, and my mother is so sick."
A white-haired man upon the corner stood,
Waiting a car. When little Robert thrust
The paper toward him, he looked kindly down,
And through his frame a sudden shiver ran,

As if the hot south wind had turned to sleet,
And pierced him through and through.   He stretched
    his hand,
And dropped it like a withered autumn leaf
Upon the child's head, asking tremulously,
"What is your name, my boy?   Tell me your name."
"Robert Earle Gray!"
                        "I knew it, yes, I knew it!
The violet eyes are Edith's, and the brow;
But the thick locks, and grave, unyielding mouth
And proud smile, are his father's.   Edith's boy,
Bearing my name too!   Edith's child, her son!
Tell me your street and number, Robert Gray."
And then, as Robert answered wonderingly,
A shining coin was dropped upon his palm,
That made his large eyes shine with speechless joy.
He faltered, "Thank you!" but the old man turned
And hailed the passing horse-car.   Robert Earle,
Pacing his lonely chamber on that night,
Felt his heart bursting with pent agony,
And from his lips there broke a heavy moan
Against the desolate silence of the night,
Like a great wave upon a barren rock:
"Edith, my rose, my darling, sick, alone,
Trodden down somewhere in the mire and slime
Of this great city—somewhere sick, alone—
Weeping alone in some close, stifling den!
My God!   My God! it need not thus have been,
If I had acted nobly, and obeyed
The inmost angel promptings of my heart.
I think if I had given a helping hand

To Walter, he had been a better man;
And I had been so happy all these years,
With Edith's tender smile to light the house,
Keeping a twelve-month bloom about the hearth,
And Edith's children climbing on my knees."
No sorrow strikes its aching roots so deep
Into the heart, as that whose seed we sow
Ourselves, in anger, pride or heedlessness.
No bitterer cry can pierce the ear of heaven
Than this: "My God, it need not thus have been,
If I had acted nobly, and obeyed
The inmost angel promptings of my heart."

So Robert Earle his lonely chamber paced
Through all the livelong night, as he had paced
It many another night. When he had heard
Of Walter's crime and sentence, he had felt
A kind of cruel triumph, muttering:
"Now surely she will come to me again,
And I will pardon her, and take her in,
And love her children as my own." Sometimes
We fail most, when we seem to triumph most,
Or triumph, when we seem the most to fail.
A year went by, and Edith did not come,
Asking his pity, pardon, or his aid.
Upon the eve of a fierce summer day,
When wild storm winds were sobbing out of sound,
In lightning-steeded clouds that, chariot-like,
On wheels of thunder, rolling lakeward went,
And out the moon burst like a lily in bloom,
Amid the dying sounds of wind and rain

And distant thunder, ringing through the night,
He thought he heard a loud and bitter cry.
The voice was Edith's, only sharp with pain:
"My father, O my father!" Robert Earle
Paused, whitening to the white edge of his hair,
And swaying like a tall pine in the blast,
Then staggered to the window, flung it wide,
And leaned his silver head into the night
Until the dripping eaves had drenched his locks,
And all his heart went out to meet that cry.
He would forgive her, find her, bring her home;
And ere he knew, he sent an answering cry
Ringing along the darkness of the night:
"Edith, my rose!" And then he started back;
It was a trick of fancy—he would wait
A little longer; she would come to him.
Beware, who drive some sweet emotion back
Upon the heart, and will not let it break
Upon the shores of action, for behold,
Its white soul-inspiration, foam-like, melts,
As it recedes into the depths again,
And new emotions, foaming, forward press.
Act 'neath the flush of purpose, like a light!—
Speak with the dew of longing in thy heart,
For there are angel touches on the will,.
Which, slighted, come no more. A year passed by,
And Edith did not come; and so to-night
Paced Robert Earle his lonely chamber through,
And waited till the tempest in his soul
Should have abated. When the first faint pulse
Of light had quickened in the purple veins

Of the far east, he reached with trembling hand,
And rang the bell: "Bring me the carriage, John!"

Came Robert to his mother joyously,
With laden arms, and in his close-shut hand
A shining heap of silver. Edith smiled,
A strange, bright smile, like a fore-radiance
Of the new dawn at hand of a new world.
She tasted not the dainty food he brought,
But drew the letter from beneath her head
And gave it unto Robert, whispering,
So softly that it seemed like a light wind
Sighing along the grass, and Robert leaned
To catch the words that trembled from her lips:
"At early morning go, deliver this.
To-night I go away, a long, long way.
Come here, my bird, and listen—I go away.
Be strong and pure and gentle; never forget
You have a noble father, who will come
Some day to claim his darlings; welcome him
With tenderest love, and gladden all his life.
Sing 'Jesus, Lover of my Soul,' my bird."
And then the little maiden, linnet-like,
Perched by the pillow, raised her tiny voice,
The human instinct of the sorrowful
Making the sweet notes quiver with a grief
But vaguely comprehended, like a cloud
That darks the sunlight of a day in June.
A splendor fell upon the dying face,
A kind of angel wonder, like the light
That well might break across an angel's face,

Who, underneath a heavenly palm-tree, smiles,
To hear across ethereal night and hush,
Some new star singing its creation hymn.
The song being ended, Edith seemed to sleep,
And Robert took, with manly tenderness,
His little sister on his knees, and rocked
Her to and fro, and hushed the childish talk
Into a quiet whisper, lest it break
The sleeper's fragile sleep. When the first pulse
Of light had quickened in the purple veins
Of the far east, then Edith woke, arose,
And stretching out her hands, as if she clasped
The hands of one before her, whispered, "Come!"
And then, as if a pitying angel stood,
Holding the soul of that last lover's kiss,
Until the fitting moment, when he leaned,
And laid it like a glory on her lips,
She smiled and murmured, "Walter, I have chosen."
Then fell back on her pillow, and, smiling, died.
Then there arose a piteous, plaintive cry,
As from young birds the hunter's cruel shot
Has left unmothered in the fragile nest,
Exposed to night and storm and heartless hands.

Within the open door stood Robert Earle,
And from his lips there broke a heavy groan,
Like a great sound of heart-break: "God, too late!"
Then, coming near, he took the little ones
Upon his heaving bosom, faltering,
"Her last words! Can you tell her very last?"
Said Robert, weeping, "Walter, I have chosen."

PART IV

RESURRECTION

Forth from his tomb at last came Walter Gray,
Threw back his head to let the soft air feel
With cool, sweet touches 'round his face and throat,
With a wild throb of life along his veins.
No angel rolled, with noiseless finger-touch,
A white stone from his sepulcher away,
But hard the heavy doors behind him clanged,
Like a loud clap of thunder, and he stood,
Drinking the golden air and sunlight—free!
And that one thought of rapture swelled his soul,
Like a pure wind that fills a snow-white sail.
So easy 'tis to glad the heart of man!
For, like a golden sunbeam through the dark,
One smile can make life sweet and liveable.
How would the world look without Edith now,
Whose smile had been in color of all clouds,
Whose voice in all the music of the waves,
Who made a part of all things unto him?
Had he forgotten when a summer day
Was dying in the arms of night and storm,
He heard the cry of Edith through the night,
So sharp and strong it pierced the heavy walls—
"Walter, O Walter, Walter!" and he cried,
Out of a weary dream, "My darling, here!"
The voice was silent now forevermore
That never by a harsh word was untuned,

But sweet with unspent kisses, like low wind
Soft with the unshed drops of summer rain.
Edith was gone; had he forgotten the night
That word of lightning pierced the prison wall,
And struck his shuddering heart with double death—
A death in death? Nay, he had not forgotten,
But life, dear God, is sweet, in spite of fire
Upon the brain, and frost upon the heart.
Some hours are sweet still, with the sweetest flown;
Some hearts are dear still, with the dearest dead;
And Walter had his little boy and girl.
That ten years seemed like a night's sleep to him,
And a night's sleep divides, like a soft hand,
A bright day from a day, like wave from wave,
And cheats old Time a little of his power.
It seemed but yesterday his little ones
Clambered like squirrels up and down his arms,
His fingers twined amid their flower-like locks;
Their little kisses moist were on his cheeks;
The music of their light, gazelle-like feet
And little laughing lips were in his ears.
The golden waves of sunlight gently beat
Against his quivering eyelids, and above,
Light clouds, with snowy fleece and windy feet,
Chased one another through the fields of heaven.

Back to the city, through old walks and ways,
Drifting and drifting, like a last year's leaf,
With no will but the wind's, so, on and on,
Upon the ceaseless tide of human life,
That writhed and twisted in and out the streets,

Alleys and tunnels, till he leaned at last
Against a granite pillar, weary and sad.
Above him rose a grand, gray, massive pile
In its gray dignity of stone and tower,
The city's latest glory, and beneath,
The pavement seemed to gently rise and sink,
In slow pulsations, timing with the lake.
Heedless of one another, and of him,
The people rushed by, each on some mad quest
Of personal gain or glory. How they jarred
And jostled one another, each one deep
In his own tangled meshes of desire,
Lost like a spider snarled in his own web.
No one would know him whom the state disnamed,
And numbered in a deep baptism of shame.

Amid the clash and clatter of the street,
Came drifting human accents rich and low—
A wave of music on a sea of sound.
Each heart-beat made a ripple in the voice
That murmured over it. He caught his breath—
Like hers, but not hers—golden tresses too!
"For Charlie's Christmas greeting when he wakes!"
The throbbing voice was saying. Walter clung
Close to the granite pillar—Christmas, then—
Christmas was coming—that which used to be
The happiest day of all the happy year.

He raised his eyes, and a familiar face
Gleamed out amid the strangeness like a light.
His heart cried out, "A friend!" as from the shore,

A shipwrecked sailor cries, "A sail, a sail!"
"Martyn, old friend!" he cried, and stretched his
    hand.
They had been friends in Walter's prosperous days,
When, condescending somewhat from his height
Of seeming affluence, he had deigned to ask
A modest loan of Walter in a strait.
The wheel of fortune, turning suddenly,
Had whirled him to the bottom, and with him,
A hundred men and women, who, unversed
In subtle trickery and slick disguise
Of wise world ways, had trusted him too much.
Then Martyn's wife was suddenly possessed
Of unguessed riches; with her jeweled hand
Turned back the wheel of fortune, lifted him
Into the public favor and social smile,
But left his trusting victims in the ruin.
Back drew the man, and ran an insolent glance
Cool, keen-edged, up and down the cowering form,
And passed on like a stranger. Walter's heart
Was bitter in his bosom. "Who is wronged,
Except my wretched self and those I love?"
So, leaning on the pillar, Walter mused,
And fancied that the lap-dogs, riding by,
With silver bells and bright embroidered coats,
Looked sideways at him as they sniffed the air.

A gentle hand was laid upon his arm,
The only gentle thing that he had met,
And Martha whispered, "This is Walter Gray."
"Hush, Martha, say it not—I have no name,"

He said, but kissed with joy the withered cheek,
All wet with tears, half sorrow, half delight.
"Forgive these tears—my heart spills over, sir."
"God bless you, Martha, for I think he led
You to me in my anguish, dear, kind soul!"
When sorrow strikes its lightning through our days,
The hearts to which we look for kindly help,
Unquestioning, as the rose to heaven for rain,
Most often will have nothing sweet to give;
While out of hearts of which we least had thought,
Burst sparkling springs of human kindliness.
"The children, Martha, tell me—what of them!
Does Aunt Maria have the children still?"
"The children, children!" Martha spoke the words,
As if they had been strange from a strange tongue:
"Ah! sir, the world keeps moving while we wait;
The roses grow on while the gardener sleeps.
Your boy and girl are man and woman now,
Both married! How you start! Yes, married well!
You've not forgotten Lucius Coventry;
Well, Robert married Lucius' daughter, Grace,
And little Elsa, his son, Lucius; yes,
Both rich and happy! They are not yours now."
"The babies married?—Why! when last I held
Their pretty, rosy faces to my breast,
Robert was twelve, and little Elsa nine.
Not mine, not mine! Ah! they will love me still.
Where are they, Martha? Let me go to them!"
"Don't seek them, sir—don't try to drag them down
From the high, sunny places where they sit;
They're rich and happy, and a little proud.

They don't remember the old nurse at all,
But they are Edith's children. Do you know,
I sometimes vex my brain with these queer things—
How little there is of the human soul,
Apart from all the places, times and things
And people that become a part of it?
Don't blame the little ones for growing proud;
The angels would grow dim and change, I think,
'Neath forces that constrain the human heart.
I love the children, but I keep away,
And if you love them, sir, you'll let them be."
"Keep from my babies—Edith's babes and mine!—"
"Ah! maybe, sir, they'd not remember you."
Walter clasped both his hands above his heart,
As if an arrow pierced it, and he reeled:
"Do we forget the loving eyes that lean,
Star-like above our cradle—love and lean,
Through all the tender dawn of infancy?
Nay, Martha, they will know and love me still."
"Ah! sir, you do not know them as I do.
Maybe they think you're dead."
                              "Nay, Martha, nay,
For I have written to them many times.
Dead people do not write, or else I think
I had had angel letters long ago."
And Walter would have smiled, had not his lips,
Unpracticed in that grace for ten long years,
Almost forgotten the sweet way of it.
"Dead people sometimes come to life again
At disagreeable times and places, sir."
"Did Aunt Maria teach them I was dead?"

"I am not sure—I think so; many times
I've picked the pieces of your letters up,
And tossed them in the fire; I think, mayhap,
She never read them to the little ones,
Telling them you were dead, for she was wise,
Was Edith's Aunt Maria, very wise."
Then Walter clasped his brow, and underneath,
His great gray eyes burned with a holy wrath.
"And Edith, Martha, what did Edith say?"
"Always the good, sir, never a bitter word.
She told the children you had gone away,
That some day you were coming home again;
And every night she had them kneel and clasp
Their little hands like folded lily buds,
And bow their heads upon them, side by side,
The dark and bright together, praying for you."
Then Walter murmured, "I *have* come again,
And I will find my pretty boy and girl."
"If you will seek them, wait a little—wait—
Tide over Christmas."
                    "Martha, wherefore wait?
Have I not waited ten long, lonely years?
Why suffer this heart-thirst another day?
I'm starving, Martha, for a crumb of love."
Then Martha laid a hand on either arm,
And turned him gently 'round, until her eyes
Looked into his steadfastly, then she spoke:
"A merry day is Christmas to the rich;
Don't spoil it for the children." Blinding flash
Of swift, white lightning; parting back the night,
An instant, and revealing heaven and earth,

Then leaving double darkness! Walter drew
His hand across his eyes as if to brush
A cobweb 'twixt him and the sunlight hung:
"My pretty boy and girl disown me?—ha!
My deepest anguish sounded not such depths.
But if they know not why I went áway,
Ah! surely they will welcome me with smiles."
Then Martha clutched her fingers on his arm,
And the large tears splashed down from cheek to
    breast:
"Oh! there's the trouble, sir, they know it all.
I meant to spare you, but you drove me to it.
The morning papers blazoned your release,
Telling your story over, coloring it,
So that the newsboys had a prosperous day."
Then Walter clasped his brow between his hands,
And turning, looked in the great window-pane.
He saw the close gray hair about the face,
All seamed and counter-seamed, the stooping form,
And then the vision faded, and he saw
A pretty room all decked with Christmas wreaths
And Christmas tokens, and a lithe young man
With richly curling locks, a happy smile
Upon his grave young mouth, and at his side
A slender woman crowned with golden hair,
Two pretty romping children at their feet,
The tender look and smile, the clasp and kiss,
The clear, unclouded lovelight all the day.
The thunder of the multitude outside
Melted into the distance, and his ears
Were filled with ringing laughter and sweet speech—

A human music sweeter to man's ears
Than angel wings beat out of silver lutes.
There came a gentle pressure on his arm:
"A crowd is gathering, sir, let us move on,
For crowds are not nice things for such as us;
Shall you not want some further talk with me?"
"I want my boy and girl!" he fiercely said.
"Homeless and wifeless, childless, nameless! God!
Has my sin called for so great punishment?"
He covered up his eyes, and sobbed aloud,
While Martha drew him gently down the street,
Striving to speak some homely words of cheer:
"Try to forget the anguish of the past,
God's bitter medicine of pain; believe
The future yet has sweet wine stored for you."
"Nay, Martha, nay, a whole eternity
Of shadowless delight can never make
Amends for such an hour of agony."
She begged that he would come and dine with her:
"I have six stalwart, rosy sons," she said,
"So that I need not toil for strangers now.
I shall be proud to have you take their hands.
Come dine with us—we shall be honored, sir,
If you will only eat a little crust
From off our table." Walter shook his head.
To joyless hearts the sight of others' joy
Makes the heart faint, and sorrow doubly sad,
And food is hard to swallow with tears for wine.
"Nay, Martha, nay, the sweetest food would choke;
I'll go and think. Farewell, dear, loving soul!"

So Walter sought out an obscure hotel,
And registered his name, And Company.
"A queer name!" said the clerk, and idly changed
The And to Andrew: "Holland, sir, or Swede?"
"Saxon!" the stranger muttered, as he caught
The key tossed to him, on his open palm.
All night he paced his chamber up and down,
Fanning a flickering purpose in his heart,
And when the white face of the morning looked
Smiling, in through the dingy window-pane,
He turned to greet it, saying, "I am resolved."

As the sad sunshine slipped along the world,
Melting its dreams,—for to the eyes that weep,
The sunshine seemeth sadder than the night,—
He trod the long streets hushed in Christmas peace.
Shone never so radiantly a Christmas sun,
But Walter's heart was full of night and storm;
Pealed Christmas laughter never so merrily,
But Walter had forgotten the way to smile.
Swift, happy feet went hurrying to and fro
On missions glad—he had a mission too—
To find his children, and to hear his doom.

It was a young man set the door ajar;
Dark, richly-curling locks, blue, splendid eyes
Under a broad, white brow, and a grave mouth,
With just a mirthful quiver at its red curves;
So like the father in his happy youth,
With glimpses of the mother here and there.
So handsome and so manly, Walter gazed,

Thrilled with a sudden ecstasy—his boy,
Robert Earle Gray, yes, Edith's son and his!
So long he gazed, that over the bright face,
A black suspicion darkened like a cloud.
He closed the door behind him while he spoke:
"What will you have, sir? I am Robert Gray."
"I knew your father, Robert, long ago,"
Came back the hollow answer from white lips,
Like a deep murmur from an ocean cave.
"I thought perhaps that you would like to know—"
"Stop there!" he cried in anger, "stop just there!
You've read the shameful story, and you've come
For money, blackmail—speak, is it not so?"
But Walter spoke not, dumb from-lips to heart.
Then Robert leaned back, and the lightnings played
From his blue, splendid eyes, while he spoke on,
As if none other listened but himself:
"I have no love, no, not a spark for him!
And wherefore should I have for such a wretch?
I have been taught to think that he was dead,
Dead with the love and honor of men's hearts
Thick on his grave as white dew from the stars.
I have believed a lie, it seems. By heaven!"
He straightened, whitening with a sudden wrath:
"'Twere better for us all if he *were* dead!
Tell me by what right, human or divine,
He comes, a skeleton of buried shame,
To stalk across the sunshine of my life?
Now if you know him, or can find him out,
Go ask of him that question!" Walter turned,
Still answering nothing, dumb from heart to lips,

The cruel word-wounds bleeding inwardly.
Robert stretched forth his hand imperiously:
"You have not said what brought you hither! Speak!"
Should Walter speak? Were it not kinder now,
Knowing his son's heart toward him, who had come,
A shadow 'twixt him and the shining sun,
To, shadow-like, in silence, glide away?
But, faint with wild heart-hunger, Walter spoke,
With all the father yearning from his eyes:
"Were *I* your father—" Robert caught the words
Up from his burning lips like sparks of fire,
That kindled a fresh anger in his breast:
"Were you my father, you would comprehend
How every breath you draw creates a mist
To darken, soon or late, into a cloud
Upon the fair horizon of my life;
And if you loved me, you would go away,
Far, far away into some lonely land,
Where you could hide forever your self and name,
Until—until you died." The beauteous face,
Unrippled by a sweet emotion, bent
Like scornful marble. Walter clinched his hands,
And tottering like a half-felled pine, he cried,
"I am your father!"
      "Aye, I thought as much!"
Robert made answer, while his youthful cheek
Whitened with fury, and his red lips twitched.
Forth Walter stretched a faltering hand, and cried,
"Robert, my boy, am I so vile a wretch
You will not take my hand in parting, once?"
But Robert heeded not the tremulous hand:

"Make no appeals to me—have I not said
I love you not; your life is but a threat,
A muttering cloud upon my sunny heaven?"
Then Walter murmured, "Robert, I will be
A kind and loving father. You are right;
I might have known, and yet I thought, I thought—
No matter what I thought." And Walter turned,
Blinded with tears of fire, and groped his way,
Half creeping, down the gleaming marble steps.
'Twere well if sound, like sight, were drowned in
   tears,
For Robert, with a merry, mocking laugh,
Made answer to a sweet voice at the door,
"Only a Christmas beggar, Gracie!" Oh!
That pricked the fainting manhood in his breast.
Hope after hope had, like a meteor, burst,
And fallen in dull gray ashes, but one star
Still through the deepening darkness softly burned—
His pretty, prattling Elsa, his sweet bird,
Who wept aloud for pity when she saw
A cripple struggling on his hands and knees
Bravely across the slippery, crowded street.
Surely the little girl had kept for him,
Burning in some dim chamber of her heart,
A little lamp of love all pure and bright,
Filled last time from a mother's dying lips,
Trimmed by the angel hand of memory.
Ah, little girl! she is a woman now,
Another man to love, but what of that?
A noble heart is never wholly filled;
Each love enlarges it to hold new love,

And deepens old affections; as the stream
Fed by new streams, must widen out its shores,
And deepen its old channel.
                          "Not at home!"
The servant sharply answered at the door.
"Away so early, and on Christmas morn?"
"Well, sir, I only meant she can't be seen."
If she but knew the suppliant at her door,
Would she not fly on swift feet winged with joy,
With bursts of ringing laughter and sweet speech?
"Tell her," he faltered, "that an old-time friend,
Who knew the family many years ago,
Is at the door, and prays to speak with her."
The maid withdrew with slow, reluctant steps,
And Walter lifted up his eyes and saw
A golden head lean from the drifted lace,
That veiled the polished window near at hand,
As from the white rim of a filmy cloud,
A star half slips. Blue, curious eyes peered out.
This second Edith was so like the first,
The first time she had dawned upon his sight,
Ripe, rosy cheeks, blue eyes and golden hair,
He scarce refrained from crashing through the pane.
The bright star disappeared behind its cloud;
Then there were footsteps, softly-closing doors,
And earnest whisperings, and through it all,
The even music of a manly voice,
And presently the maid, returning, spoke:
"My mistress says she cannot speak with you,
And bids you state your business." Did she feel
A shadow hovering near on that bright morn?

Was she in league with that hard, bitter world?
Where was the winsome, loving, laughing child,
So tender that she wept to wound a worm?
A storm of grief and anger swept aside
All the restraints of reason and of will:
"Tell her her father stands without the door,
And asks to speak with her." There came a sound
Of footfalls light as dropping autumn fruit,
Of rustling robes like wind-blown autumn leaves,
And as a scared bird from the thicket flies,
Another listener, from behind the door,
Glided along the hall and up the stairs;
And from above dropped down a sweet bird voice,
As sweet and pure as dewy morning notes
By happy, soaring linnet careless dropped,
From vortices of rosy mist and cloud,
Through golden rhythms of light upon the world.
"Susie," it twittered, "send that man away;
Tell him I have no father." Walter leaned
Forward, and sent a strong and shuddering cry
Ringing among the rosy, perfumed halls:
"Elsa, my bird, come down, come down to me;
For the old tyrant hunter waits for you!"
That was the cry that wooed her baby feet
To the mad evening frolic; now it rang,
All sharp and shivering, with the startling sound
Of something costly breaking. A heart broke.
Then fell the hush of deep dismay which comes
After the crash of ruin, then a moan,
The tender sound of weeping and low sobs,
With whispered pleadings—she is coming; joy!

The child is coming! Walter stretched his arms.
Oh! now is recompense!   Hark!—a man's voice,
Stern and commanding: "Susie, close the door;
The fellow's crazy; have John drive him off!"
And Susie whispered with an honest tear,
Of pity shining on her rosy cheek,
"Her husband!" as she softly closed the door.
Then Walter's reason faltered, and his brain
Was full of flitting shapes and jangling sounds,—
The silver crash of waters on the shore,
The jostling, staring multitude, the glare
Of gorgeous windows, and the idle jest
And laughter of gay people, and the whirl
Of pleasure's giddy wheels, and miles and miles
Of crowded streets, and then long, lonely ways,
With scattered houses and bare, bloomless fields,
And only one thought beating in his brain—
To press his lips to Edith's grave, and die.

And when at last the gleaming granite shaft,
On which was carved the name of Robert Earle,
And on the right, the name of Edith Earle,
And on the left, the name of Edith Gray,
Flashed coldly on his burning sight, there lay
A shining sunset cloud across the west,
Stretched like a splendid angel at full length,
Within the dusky splendor of whose smile
Glistened the white spires of the city of sleep.
Then Walter, falling prone on Edith's grave,
Lay motionless, except for the faint breath
That stirred his pale lips, while the noiseless hours

Trod softly through the darkness, till at last,
The beautiful, slow-footed dawn approached.
The dimming moon like a strained eyeball stared,
Until a light cloud, sliding down the sky,
Like a white eyelid folded over it.
Then ached his heart with a returning sense
Of agony, a conscious bruise and strain,
As if it had been crushed 'neath sorrow's heel,
Until too numb to feel its own great hurt.
He pressed his pale lips close to the cold grave,
And cried, with a loud, agonizing cry,
"Edith!" and once more—"Edith!" and again—
"Edith!" beseechingly, as if he thought
The mighty anguish of the voice of love,
Entreating through the silence of the grave,
Could strike through even the dreamless ear of death.
Only the faint stir of the faded grass
Made gentle answer, and a withered leaf
Came quivering down beside him on the grave.
Ungenerous nature left earth's naked limbs
Without their timely robe of snowy grace.
There was a crystal silence everywhere,
Save when a young wind, like a viewless bird,
With frosty pinions winging through the night,
Would light among the branches, panting there,
Shaking the skeletons of the dead leaves
That clung about the branches. Walter rose,
Seeing far off and dim a radiant thought,
Hovering upon the brain's edge distantly,
Too far and dim to trace its glorious shape,
Advancing and retreating like a star.

Straining his gaze lest it should slip from view,
He wandered blindly on and on, until
He heard the silver lapping of the lake
Close by his feet.   And far off in the south,
A cloud of thick smoke sprinkled through with
    lights,
Showed where the city, in unquiet sleep,
Lay breathing heavily in feverish dreams,
And over it the still, star-trodden skies.
Some great thoughts seem to burst into the brain
Full-orbed, like heaven's new stars, but only seem;
For all a man hath ever done or been,
His slightest thought, emotion, word or deed,
All works of God, of angels, or of men,
The whole weight of the past eternity,
Bears down upon the moment as it comes,
Shaping resistlessly its thought and deed.
Walter looked out upon the darkling lake,
Bounded by pale fog flecked with glimmering lights,
As strong and swift and sleepless, the great boats
Backward and forward flew like carrier birds,
With olive twigs of commerce in their beaks,
And thought some strange new thoughts of life and
    things:
"It must be happiness is good for man;
His heart, hot-lipped, thirsts so for one deep draught
Of life's joy, that, like eucharistic wine,
An angel seems to pass from lip to lip,
That each may simply touch the rosy rim,
And keep the taste to smile by in his dreams.
No fear the soul will drink so deep of bliss

That it will sink in languor and soft dreams,
Since life is life, and death is always death,
And 'twixt these the unthinking elements,
Blind lightnings and deaf thunders, thoughtless winds,
Unfeeling waters and dumb earthquake shocks,
Play with man's delicate senses and fair limbs,
As with insentient rocks and trees and flowers.
Say not that trouble falleth a white flame,
From hands divine, all-tender and all-wise,
To burn souls white! We're done with that dead creed,
Since many hearts are crisped and scarred and scathed,
Where one walks glistening, unsinged through the flames.
I think God smiles upon our human smiles,
And man brews most of his own bitterness,
From harvests of his own heart's selfishness.
The century's cry is not from man to God
For the divine compassion and reprieve,
But from the outraged heart of man to man,
For simple justice. Thou, God, make us wise
Enough to know the happiness of each
Is measured by the happiness of all,
As the most kingly sun that ever swayed
The fairest constellation in the heavens,
Moves only to the music of all worlds,
Vibrating to the touch of unseen stars.
Since the first time man gazed on sun and cloud,
Breathed breath of flowers, and listened to low winds,

And himself made the music of sweet speech,
And sinned and loved and labored and learned tears,
His heart has whispered to him prophetwise:
"'Tis thou that sittest at the forge of time,
With iron music and with flakes of fire,
Beating thine own fate from the glowing years;
Thou forgest thine own fetters for thy feet.'
So with wild dreams and blood and tears and fire,
With thrones and anarchy and social schisms,
In hope and fear and anguish, he has striven
To build a city, whose strong, glistening walls
Shall make it ever inaccessible
To human selfishness, the one great foe
Of human happiness; and when one falls,
He searches for another, loftier site.
So, through the gloom of ages he has gone
Groping his way from shining height to height,
Like some blind angel lost in ether darks,
Feeling his doubtful way from star to star,
Knowing the good, but knowing not the way
To best achieve it."
      Walter raised his eyes,
And lo, heaven shone like a great amethyst
On God's forefinger. "Help me, God," he prayed,
"To send some golden sunbeam down the dark,
One shaft of sunlight quivering through the night
Of the storm-threatened future; let me break
Some pathway open, that shall one day lead
Down to the feet of morning through all tears,
And I shall live, and have a joy in life,
The joy that comes through doing of a thing

That's noble in the teeth of human scorn."
When up the sun rose like a lake of fire
Out of a lake of water, Walter stretched
His hands toward Edith's grave, and cried, "Farewell!
Farewell, beloved! I take a second bride,
And name and being forevermore are merged
In this, my second love—Humanity."

[NOTE: I am indebted to Mr. Collins Shackelford's sketch in an issue of the *Evening News* in December, 1889, for some of the incidents in Part IV of this book.—THE AUTHOR.]

BOOK II
THE SLAVE GIRL

PART I

FREEDOM

It lay, that splendid city by the lake,
'Neath all the summer splendor of blue skies—
A blue as fresh and stainless and unsoiled
As if a band of cherubs sent from heaven,
Had washed it up with white clouds dipped in dew.
Even where the city's heart beat loud and fast
With the returning pulses of the day,
The heavy smoke, upbreathed from panting lungs
Of myriad engines, seemed to shrink abashed
From the pure heaven, as a polluted soul
Shrinks back in awe from spotless innocence.
The river like a headless giant lay—
Headless, but heaving still with torpid life.
Along the languid arms and sluggish sides,
Full in the monstrous armpits ceaseless swarmed
The ever-building, building human ants.
Not long since the first big, white-winged canoe
Came flying o'er the blue, astonished lake,
And lo, the liquid music which rude oars
Were beating out of tuneful wave-harps, ceased,
And the wild songs of savage love and hate
Died in sad echoes on the lonely shore.
Then faded from the waters the bright dream
Of glancing bark-canoes and waving oars,
And scarlet-shirted oarsmen, to and fro
Waving in time to song and stroke of oar.

Not long since, like a beauteous thing of life,
With neither beating oars nor waving wings,
With throbbing heart and breath, almost a brain,
Defying will of winds and waves' caprice,
Came walking o'er the waves majestically,
The conquering steamer in whose white wake sprang,
Like Aphrodite radiant from the foam,
The spirit of the new age, and behold,
Where the wild onion waved upon the shores
Of the "Chicaugou," flowing sluggishly,
Stretch miles and miles of dockage, and no more
The echo of a savage melody
Finds room 'mid roar of traffic night and day.
And now the languid river, like the bond
Which held the twins of Siam, firmly binds
In one the threefold city—triple birth
Of the young century, that, now grown gray,
Stands on its radiant evening's golden edge,
Leaning upon its staff, and with a smile,
Half triumph, half mysterious prophecy,
Looks eastward where the sweet, prophetic glow
Of the new dawning century appears,
Faint flushing up the heavens.
                              So it lay
Anointed with the sunrise, like a queen,
That splendid city by the lake, whose waves
Were in their gentlest mood, and softly purred
Against the quiet shore, while eastward far,
It dimpled faintly, like the cheek of one
Who sleeps and dreams, and all unconscious smiles.
As shoreward surges an incoming tide,

The refluent sea of life rolled cityward,
Like heart-blood swift returning on the heart,
And the long streets like shuddering arteries beat.
Now high in heaven pushed the golden sun,
And quiet fell upon the wide, fair streets,
Where smiled serene and stately in the sun,
With mutual congratulations, each
Upon the other, calm, complacent smiles,
The rich men's dwellings. Oh! the hearts of men
Mix with the city's brick and mortar. Aye,
And cry out of the pavements and the walls,
The things men strive to strangle out of sound.

This morning walked two children hand in hand,
Beside the gray sea wall, against which laughed
The happy little waves like gleeful babes,
And after them a woman meanly clad,
But with a gentle grace, meek, mournful eyes,
Gently beseeching, unresentful, yet
Mutely reproachful, like dumb creatures' eyes;
A mouth 'round which a subtle sweetness lurked,
So sweet that all life's bitterness had failed
To make it bitter. Any one had said,
"The mother of both children, and the boy
Has seen eight summers, and his sister, ten."
Because the boy was small and slightly built,
With cheeks like lilies, bloomless, and with eyes
Like timid violets, and a wide, white brow
With tremulous blue veins crossed, and clinging
  waves
Of brown hair flowing 'round it; while the girl

Betrayed in rounded limbs and ruddy cheeks,
In restless, raven curls and dark eyes' gleam,
How leaped the rosy tides of strong, sweet life,
Unchecked by pain or passion, through glad veins.
Twice gentle were her gentle words and ways,
As of an elder sister unto him,
But both were ten in that rare month of June,
And only Magia was the child of her
Who seemed a kindly mother unto both.
Sweet Magia, who, like some flowers that bloom,
Though starved of dew and sunlight and soft showers,
Had kept her sweet life without blast or blight,
Defiant of all gloom and stagnant air.

Close where the river, reeking in its slime,
Crawls green and venom-breathing, like a snake,
Where virtue, life and love, and rent are low,
Lived Magia with her mother in a room
Bare of all luxury except the flow
Of bright, impartial sunlight, all untaxed,
Upon the spotless floor, and on a shelf
A few worn volumes. Here had Magia lived
A twelvemonth with her mother, whose white face
Was set with the strange patience of mute vows
Against the social order that compelled
Her to its cold embrace and forced her still
To please its idle humors, though divorced
Forever from it by its cruelty.
That mother had a secret in her eyes,
And kept her eyelids drooped to shut it in.
In vain the frowsy women of the house

Had leered and jeered upon her, calling out
That the fine lady better get herself
A brown-stone front upon the avenue,
And live with the fine people like herself,
Too good to speak to poor folk; but she kept
Upon her quiet way, and paid no heed
To taunts of misery, or cold neglect
Of wealth and happiness, asked naught, gave naught,
Loved nothing but the little loving thing,
The sweet child Magia, before her eyes
Like a live picture of her fair, dead self.
Nor ever Magia played upon the street
With the thick swarms of children that poured out
From hive-like tenements, and cursed and quarreled,
Aping the older ones in perfect way,
But always dressed in bright and dainty clothes,
She played alone about the barren room.
No toys had little Magia to beguile
The long, long hours of childhood, for so far
The mother's heart was swept from that bright isle
Of fairy groves and grottoes and white rills,
By life's wild tempest, that she had forgot
The pretty, foolish fancies of a child.
But Magia needed nothing, for she watched
The white steam clouds upfloating, and she played
With gleaming suds, that from her mother's hands
Fell off like fairy snow in some rare clime
Produced by warm south wind and summer sun,
Or tried to break the golden lines of dust
Thridding the rays of sunlight, or else played
At gathering up the sunbeams from the floor,

Or laughed to see the raindrops leap and dance
Upon the window sill, or even sometimes
Threw back her head and clasped her little hands,
And burst in peals of laughter long and sweet.
Whereat her mother faintly smiled and said,
"What pleases you, my Magia?" and the child,
In pauses of the music, out of breath,
Made answer, "There is something in me laughs."
It was the ecstasy of perfect life,
That like an angel leaped and clapped its wings
With sounds of rhythmic sweetness in the soul,
And silver bursts of laughter from the lips
That rippled unrestrainedly.
                              Never yet
Had Magia played with children, or exchanged
The pretty speech of childhood with a child.
But in the ceaseless flitting to and fro
Of souls from tenement to tenement,
Amid the toiling populace, like birds
That nest but for a season, in the spring
There came a noisy pair and took the room
Dingy and dismal at the long hall's end.
The pair had one pale child, a boy who grew
Too slowly and not strong or straight.   Perchance
The mother, in a drunken stupor, dropped
The babe and jarred life's delicate machine
Out of its fine adjustment, after which
The wheels of life ran painfully, and jarred
Sometimes on one another.   Oftentimes,
Through thin partitions came discordant sounds
Of drunken quarrels and scuffling, flying curse

And flying missile, hideous laughter blent
With the low, piteous sobbing of a child.

One day when little Magia played alone
Within the soft May sunshine on the floor,
The din of blows and curses grew so fierce,
She gently set the door ajar and stood
Peering along the dim hall. Suddenly
The door flew wide, and with a piteous cry,
That like the frightened bleat of a lost lamb
On which the wolf has pounced with savage snarl,
Rang sharply down the passage, the pale child
Was flung out like a heap of rubbish, full
Against a ragged corner of the wall,
Which marked the white brow with a crimson gash.
Then little Magia's heart beat loud and fast,
Swelling with an emotion strange and new,
Like the inrush of waters warm and sweet
From newly opened fountains. 'Twas not joy
Nay, nor yet sorrow, but betwixt these two,
Tender and warm and sweet and undefined,
Like mist 'twixt clouds and sunshine a May morn—
Divinest pity. Swift as summer breeze
Through grassy lane, fled Magia down the hall,
And flung her dimpled arms around the boy.
As if an angel, stooping to her ear,
Whispered the heavenly prompting, Magia cried,
"Come, little brother, come and live with me.
You shall play with my sunbeams, and shall have
The half of all my good things." Then she drew
Him unresisting through the open door

Into the soft May sunshine, and she told
Him all the bright things in her little life—
Her sunshine and her snow-flakes and her rain,
And how upon one day in all the week,
If nature lent one bright in all the seven,
Her mother took her to the cool, green park,
And told her wondrous tales, or read to her
Out of some book. He might go with them now.
So Magia prattled till the pallid mouth
Began to curve and quiver with the light
Of an approaching smile, as a spring flower,
Chilled by the night-wind, trembles with the glow
Of an approaching sunbeam. Then he laughed,
And startled by the music hid his face;
But Magia leaped with rapture at the sound,
Which changed at once the simple melody
Of her own childish laughter evermore
To double-toned, deep sweetness, never more
The single note, but ever the complex chord.
She tried to pull the fragile hands apart,
That, like the petals of a folded bud,
Unwilling to be parted, tightly clung,
And being stronger, forced the delicate palms,
And gathered up her lips into a kiss.
But he sat unresponsive, knowing not
Whatever a kiss could mean. Then, like a flash,
An angel intuition, a warm glow
Of the May sunshine from the hills of heaven,
It broke on Magia's soul, the strange perhaps,
That when the angels taught this little soul
The alphabet of heaven that it must learn

To fit it for the world, they had forgot
The happy angel instinct of a kiss.
And so she taught him what it seemed to her
The angels had forgotten—its sweet lore,
Its fashion and its meaning. As he heard,
His eyes with wisdom and with wonder grew,
And in their far blue depths crept up a light,
A shining like the dawn upon the lake,
And kindled like a sunrise in the soul.
A shadow on the happy sunlight fell;
A discord crossed the harmony of speech,
And Magia's mother, with rebuking words,
Frowning upon the strange child, bade him go.
But Magia clung about her mother's neck
With passionate pleadings, while the stranger hid
His frightened white face in the crimson folds
Of little Magia's skirt. Meanwhile she told
His pitiful story, and the mother bent,
Uncovered the stained brow, and gently asked,
"What might your name be?"
                          "Manley!"
                                   "Manley what?"
"Manley Marcellus." "Stay," the mother said,
"Stay till they seek you." Lo, a woman's shriek,
Unto a two-edged sharpness terror-whet,
Pierced through the thin walls of the startled house,
And for a fresh sensation famishing,
Thither the people flocked, like clamorous birds
About a carcass, finding what they craved—
A woman reeking in her own warm blood,
And, crouching on the floor, his crazy brain

Sobered by shock of his own violent deed,
The man, the woman's mate, clutched in his hand
A knife red with the same blood. After that,
The inquest and the trial, and one day
A man was hung for murder, late in June,
Wife-murder. All was done, done and passed by,
Leaving upon the restless social sea
No firmer impress than a stone far cast
Upon the heaving bosom of the lake,
And no one sought the child, or paused to ask
If child had been.
     So little Manley stayed,
And Magia's heart was brimmed with new delight,
Believing he was hers to keep and guard;
Because a noble nature, being twice strong,
And yet twice tender, joys to spend itself
In loving service and sweet sacrifice,
Yearns to be leaned upon, and to uphold.
"A year this June day," little Magia said,
"Since little brother came!" The mother smiled
And answered, "It shall be a holiday."
And so the children played among the trees
Of one cool green oasis left by men
In the great city desert of blank stone.
Often, as they were clambering up a knoll
Or flight of steps, she reached her hand to him,—
To her it was so natural to help.
They sometimes rested by the mother's knees
And listened to some story they would weave
Into their own bright world. So when they heard
The old Norse legend—how the world was wrought

Out of a mighty giant's frame—they lay
And watched the white-cloud-brains drift lazily
In the great skull that formed the heaven's blue.
 vault,
And guessed what lightning thoughts and thunder
 dreams
Were hidden in their white folds; wondered too
If the blue lake that once had been his blood
Still quivered with his pulse's ebb and flow.
So, like a snow-flake from the hills of time,
Melted that June day quickly out of sight.

Now as the golden sun was falling fast,
And they were drawing figures on the sand,
A flock of noisy children, whose young lips
Were deft with curses as with sugar-plums,
Thither came thronging at the sunset hour.
A splendid mastiff, like a tawny lion,
Bounded among them. One had brought a stick,
And waving it on high, cried, "Fetch it, Jack!"
And flung it far as his young arm could throw.
Into the shining water, lo! a splash,
And a dark form amid the white caps plunged,
And struck out like a swimmer skilled and strong.
A breathless silence reigned upon the shore,
Unbroken till a wild, triumphant shout
Greeted the noble swimmer as he leaped
All dripping from the foam, with stick in mouth,
Shaking his shaggy sides till showers of spray
Scattered the laughing children right and left.
Then Manley, with his blue eyes luminous,

His little heart with boyish rapture swelled,
Clapped his small hands and shouted with delight.
A boy with heavy frame and shaggy locks,
With dull, unthinking face that spoke a heart
More brute than human, such a heart as finds
No pleasure half so sweet as giving pain,
Pointed his finger at the child and cried,
"The hunchback! ha! the hunchback!" Came a rush
Of scarlet to the pale face from the heart,
And swift returning on the heart again,
A twofold whiteness left in the white face.
Her dark eyes gathering lightning Magia stood;
Her red cheeks gathering crimson, then she sprang
Upon the cruel boy and bore him down;
Her dimpled knee upon his chest, she rained
The hot blows fast and fierce about his head.
The rest, delighted by the novel sport,
Shouted and clapped their hands and cheered her
    on,
Jeering their fallen comrade lustily.
I think she would have killed him, but a cry,
A sweet, pathetic, passionate, pleading cry,
Sounded above the tumult, "Magia!"
Then quickly Magia sprang to Manley's side,
And with their arms about each other twined,
They passed from sight amid the waving trees,
Amid the loud applause and cruel taunt,
"Whipped by a girl!" hurled at the fallen foe.
They sat themselves upon a grassy knoll
And Magia raised a flushed and eager face:
"Say, did I grieve you, brother, was I wrong?

Speak to me, little brother, was I wrong?"
But Manley answered nothing, in his face
The solemn revelation-light of pain,
Revealer of mysterious depths of life.

Behold the soul is born in a deep sleep,
A calm unconsciousness of life and time,
But Fate, or an appointed angel, sets
And winds up the alarm which, at the hour,
Peals sharp and shrill across the brain. The soul
Awakes, starts up, and knows that it has slept.
Some are awakened in the early dawn,
When stars are faint, and morning is not yet.
They rise alone amid the dim and chill
And hear the quiet breathing of the souls
That still are sleeping. So on that June day
The soul of Manley heard its rude alarm,
And started up half blind with light, and deaf
With strange confusion, like one suddenly,
From cold, mute space swept in upon the sun.
Seeing the revelation in his face,
But understanding nothing, Magia lay,
Her cheek against his hand, until at last
The mother sought and found them lying there,
Like a fresh rose and lily on the grass.
"We're tired playing," Magia sweetly said,
Forestalling questions, and they rose and went.

PART II

SLAVERY

It was the hour of moonrise, and the moon
Lay like a silver island of the blest,
Without a ripple on its peaceful shores.
Then Magia and Manley sat and spoke
In quiet whispers, while the mother slept,
Who lay half stricken by a dread disease,
As if death, like an executioner,
Striking with tremulous hand but half achieved
His fatal task. Near by the children sat,
And 'round them fell the moonlight soft as sleep,
And bright as down dropped from an angel's breast.
Said Magia, "Little brother, I will go,
And earn our bread and clothes, for I am strong."
Then Manley's pale cheek flushed, and in his voice
Was the soft quivering sound of unshed tears:
"Call me not *little* brother; *I* am strong.
I will go with you, Magia, and work too.
I *will* not, like a baby, stay at home."
As if their soft words pierced her fragile dream,
The sleeper stirred, and stretched her one live hand,
Clasping the children's clasped hands fast in hers:
"Ah, what is virtue? Is it not the strength
By which we stand steadfast against the wrong?
The slender cord which never felt a strain,
And never snapped, shall it be counted strong,
The while the splendid anchor that has stood

A century of mighty tug and strain,
Yet breaks at last and wrecks the gallant ship,
Is counted weak?   Hark, my sweet Magia—
White as thy thoughts so shall thy garments be.
Yes, if thy thoughts be pure, then shalt thou pass
Through all pollution unpolluted.   Yea,
As fire unto asbestos, unto thee
Will all corruption be.   Even more—thy touch
Will purify the vileness, and thy robes,
Gleaming with threefold whiteness from the filth,
Come shaming the mock purity of those
Who sit in high, clean places.   Magia, go,
You and your brother; earn us bread and clothes.
I still have one strong hand to serve myself,
And make and mend the garments for you both."

So Magia and Manley, hand in hand,
Upon the scorching stones went up and down,
From street to street, to factories, stores and shops,
Asking for work.   Most often there was none,
But sometimes Magia's rosy, dimpled face
That, like a flower washed in the morning dew,
Which neither heat nor cold had power to wilt,
Would make one turn and look again and say,
"We may have room for you, but not for him."
"He is my brother," Magia sweetly said,
"And we must work together.   Thank you, sir."
Then Magia's dimpled fingers tightlier twined
Through Manley's, and they meekly went their way,
Until at last they found a place for both.

Then Magia and Manley, hand in hand,
Went into serfdom meekly, joyously.
And all day long, amid the jostling throng
That steamed with summer heat, and filled the air
With stifling odors, mingled with the scent
Of mold and mildew from the damaged stuff
The eager rabble, wrangling over, dragged
Hither and thither, drawn like silly moths
By flaming lies which promised something fine
For foolish prices, only to be burned,
And still be drawn again, again be burned—
All day amid the ceaseless din of gain
And bargain, in the fierce electric glare,
Ever the little feet fled up and down.
And everywhere the sweet child Magia came,
Her face a blossom brimmed with morning sun,
Like flickering sunbeams on the pallid lips
Of other little serfs, broke timid smiles,
For there was morning dew upon her brow,
A dream of mountain sunshine in her eyes;
The summer wind breathed in her restless curls;
Each motion was a hint of rustling leaves,
Her laugh the echo of a waterfall.
Oft when the tall slave-driver's searching eyes
Were turned another way, although they seemed
To look all ways at once—sharp, baleful eyes,
Deep set in hueless cheeks, like embers burned
Low, and half buried in gray ashes,—then,
If little Magia saw a fragile child
Beneath a beastly burden staggering,
She sprang and lent her young arm's dimpled strength

To bear the heavy burden to its place;
She, being so fleet and light of foot, regained
Quickly all time thus lost in loving deeds.
So there are hearts that live too fast for time,
And fill with kindly deeds and helpful words,
The golden interstices up, which lie
Between the lazy minutes.
      Bessie drooped
Her shining head until the yellow curls,
Falling low forward, veiled her face and eyes,
That none might see her weeping. Then she wept,
For Bessie's mother was but two days dead.
The tears fell flashing through the yellow hair,
Like rain through sunshine. Magia turned aside,
And kissed the tender eyelids dripping wet
Like leaves with summer showers, the pallid cheek
Like a red rose washed white with too much rain.
Around them gathered soon an eager group
Of pitying children, when a sudden crack,
Like dry sticks struck together in the air,
Caused them to leap and startle like wild fawns
Scared from the thicket, flying fleet and far.
Fast the pursuer followed, and he smote
His dry palms as he drove the frightened flock
Before him.
    Ever through the twice long days
The brave child Magia kept a loving watch
Over her fragile brother, guarding him
From wrong and insult, sometimes helping him
Perform some task too heavy for his strength,
When she could do it slyly. When he lost

The pennies saved for noontide bread and tea,
She gave him hers and said, without a blush,
"I found them, brother, where you let them fall;"
And to her own pure conscience answering said,
"Because I am so strong, and he so frail."
Oh, white deceit of angels, falsehood fair,
Oh, generous lie that shames the selfish truth!
Use is the grace and glory of the world.
Justice and honor, truth and purity,
Are merged in one white splendor—human use;
And many a lie has had so white a soul,
And worn such beautiful garments of chaste love,
That the cold, naked, unavailing truth
Has humbly bowed herself and kissed its feet,
As, like an angel beautifully clothed
And loftily crowned, it came from the soul's height,
Serving divinest purposes. For naught
Is ever good or evil in itself.
The purpose is the spirit and the power.
In the white hand of purity all things
Which men have deemed unchaste, turned to chaste
    ends,
Glisten with angel grace and purity.

The air was heavy with the August heat,
And sickening exhalations from the throng.
She saw him tugging at a heavy sack
That would have taxed a strong man's strength that
    day,
His blue eyes straining wide, the purple veins
Large on his forehead, where the drops of pain

And weakness gathered, his pale lips apart,
His delicate nostrils quivering.   Suddenly
A crimson jet burst from them and splashed down
Upon the white hands.   Magia reached his side,
Careless of angry word or ugly frown,
And lent her tender strength to move the weight.
As if a rude wind hurled a naked bough
From some dead tree, and smote her tingling cheek,
It reddened with a sudden angry blow:
"Who bade you do his work?   Go mind your own.
If he's not able, we will send him home
To help his mother.   Get to business, girl!"
Then Manley's eyes were full of flash and fire.
Like a poor little bird, confused and stunned,
That dashes blindly at a blank stone wall,
He would have beat his life out on the man,
But Magia clasped his trembling hands and said,
"It didn't hurt me, brother, do not mind."
And, smiling at him, darted through the throng,
As if a sunbeam fled along the world,
Forgotten by the setting sun, nor chilled,
Nor dimmed, nor frightened by the shades of night.

"I wish I could have killed him, Magia,"
He said at night, while Magia, like a bird,
Flew here and there, and made the little room
With cleanliness and order blossom forth.
And Manley followed her, where'er he could
Lending a helping hand.   "Oh! that is wrong.
Perhaps he only did what he was bid."
"But, Magia, I think there are two ways

Of doing every duty—one that's sweet
And one that's hard and bitter. The sweet way
Will make our duty sweet to every one.
The hard way, hard to others, though to us
It have the pleasure of a duty done."
"Sweet Magia," the mother said, and reached
Her feeble hand to twist a live, bright curl
That seemed to breathe and stir on Magia's brow,
"Come smooth my pillow; kiss me; that is sweet.
Each night I look at you and smile to see
Your cheeks are no less dimpled, round and red.
But even plants that flourish in the dark
Must have the air. The breeze is from the lake;
The night is sweet and cool; the stars are bright.
Go with your brother out and breathe the air."
"O mother, I would rather stay with you.
To morrow we will go a half hour soon,
And see the sun upon the lake and breathe
The pure wind blowing from it washed in foam."
So in accord with Magia's word they went.
She tossed her curls back toward the morning sun,
And waved her dimpled arms and leaped and laughed:
"See, Manley, how I run to meet the spray.
O brother, what a lovely world it is!"
"Yes, Magia, if people were but kind!"
"If we are kind and good, why should it mar
The beauty of the world when men are bad?"
"If people have been wicked or unkind,
It takes the golden color from the sun,
And makes the bluest sky look dull and gray."

"O brother, it is never so to me.
If people have been cruel, then I look
At the sweet sunlight; that is always kind.
The sky is pure; the stars are always true;
They fill me with sweet comfort."
       "Magia,
Nature is sometimes wicked and unkind.
She often hurts us or else those we love."

The long and beauteous autumn by the lake
Had passed away. With loud and blustering breath
The winter came up howling from the sea,
Clipping the' days' bright locks with frosty shears.
Through all the morning little Manley drooped.
At noontime Magia turned and saw him climb
With slow and painful steps the long, steep stairs.
Unmindful of the printed card which hung
Upon the wall, prohibiting the "cash"
From taking hands when climbing up the stairs,
She turned and clasped her brother's hand in hers,
And so they climbed together, hand in hand.
At top of stairs a sharp glance pierced her through,
And held her trembling like a humming-bird
Upon a tyrant's bodkin: "If you please,"
Said Magia sweetly, "brother is not well."
The thin lips of the overseer laughed,
A laugh that crackled like a burning brier:
"Is that our business, brazen, insolent girl?
We do not keep a sanitarium.
You've been transgressing long enough. Now take
Your brother home and nurse him." His pale lips

Curled slowly backward from his gleaming teeth,
Like sneering waves that curl back from white rocks
Where they have wrecked brave ships.
                                    So up and down
Went Magia and Manley, hand in hand,
Through the long streets, the bitter, biting wind
Driving them to and fro like tufts of down.
And often they were rudely turned away,
And often, looking at the rosy face
Of little Magia, one would say, "Perhaps
We have a place for you, but not for him."
"He is my brother," Magia sweetly said,
"We must have work together." So they went
Until the gray wings of the winter eve
Began to early fold, and then they came
To a great factory where cloaks were made.
Here was a place for both the boy and girl.
Here Magia sat and sewed the long day through,
While Manley stood and pressed the finished work.
The room was large and low and faintly lit,
And here the little slave girls sat all day,
Patient and pale, their pretty heads bent low,
Almost against the work upon their knees,
Straining to see the stitches as they sewed.
The air was thick with dust and lint, and scent
Of many colored dyes, and tainted breaths.
The din of flying shuttles, and the click
Of busy needles, and the roar of wheels,
Made up the long monotony of sound.
No happy speech or innocent laughter struck
A chord of sweetness through the loud discord,

For silence was the iron law, unless
The overseer with the plump, pink cheeks
And silken brown mustache, and locks that curled
In hyacinthine beauty 'round his brow,
Was called to leave his post unsentineled;—
Then Rosy straightened up her flaxen head
And crooked little shoulders, while she hummed
An old hymn tune or ballad of the street.
Once Bertha leaned her arms on Magia's knees,
Saying, "You will not keep red cheeks like that,
If you stay in the Slave Hole. I work hard,
And only earn enough to pay the rent,
Nothing for shoes.. See how my toes peep out.
They'd like to gnaw the flesh off of our bones,
Then keep the bones for making penny soup.
Say, Magia, tell me, do you think God knows
About the Slave Hole? Do you think he cares
About our backaches?"
      "Surely," Magia said,
Uplifting the fresh blossom of her face,
Brimmed with the happy sunlight of a smile,
Its calyx of dark ringlets falling back,
"Why else I see no use of all the world.
Why should the flowers eat sunlight and drink dew,
The sky and sea change colors hour by hour,
The winds and waves make music, but for us?
And why for us unless God cares? I think
There must be flights of angels every day
From heaven to earth, and back again to heaven,
To bring us good and carry back our needs."
Then Rosy laughed and kicked her ragged shoes:

"What good are angels loafing round in heaven,
Playing on harps? I wish they'd come and sew
One of my shoes and patch the other. Ho!
They ought to substitute a little while
In Slave Hole, and give us poor souls a turn
At the green fields and streams of Paradise."
Said Bertha, leaning still on Magia's knees,
"I wish they'd come and sew this facing on,
My back aches so, and let me rest an hour."
"Oh! let me play at angel for a while,
And sew it on!" the sweet child Magia cried.
"And what of *your* work, Magia? Don't you know
They pay by piece in Slave Hole, not by time?"
"Oh, when I'm working for myself, I work,
But when I work for others, then I play."
Still went the days, and still the roses lived
In Magia's cheek, nor seemed to fade or droop.
As if the brave persistence of their bloom
Angered the pink-cheeked overseer, he seized
Each cruel chance to give her a harsh word,
Rebuke her if her eyes were off her work,
Or rudely bid her rip the long day's task.
And once his fat, white fingers clutched her curls,
And forced the small head toward the trembling
     knees.
Grasping the pretty shoulders with both hands,
He crushed them rudely forward, crying, "Jade,
You cannot do your work and sit so straight."
The brave child Magia uttered not a word,
Although her heart was bleeding. For herself
Another master might have soon been found,

For she had willing hands and strong, swift feet,
But Manley was so frail 'twas hard to find
Another place for him, and for his sake
She could bear any wrong or cruelty.

All day the dull sound of the iron smote
On Magia's tender heart, and oftentimes
When there was no one standing sentinel,
She slipped away and stood in Manley's place,
Pushing the heavy iron to and fro
Amid the clouds of vapor, while he tried . .
To rest his weary arms and aching back.
The little Rosy shaped her pretty lips
To make a low, peculiar sound, which served
As danger signal, when the foe approached,
Which, Magia hearing, bird-like, noiseless flew
Into her place and bent above her work.
And now the April days returned—the days
Of tearful sunshine and of sunny showers.
A flaxen head was missing: "Where is Rose?"
The whisper ran, "She's sick." Her place was filled,
As wave succeeds to wave, and no one seeks
The little wave that ran along the shore
And sparkled in the sun an hour ago.
As Magia stood upon a sweet, warm day,
Pressing a heavy garment, Manley cried,
His blue eyes full of pleading, "Do not stay.
There's no one now to warn you. I am strong."
"O brother, see the drops upon your face,
And I am tired sitting all day long."
While Magia spoke, a rude hand grasped her arm,

And flung her back so hard against the wall,
She staggered, dizzy with the sudden shock,
Nor the loud words of harsh dismissal heard.
But Manley put his little hand in hers,
And drew her forth into the gentle rain
That fell upon their young heads like soft tears
Out of the tender but unclouded sky,
As from a gracious blue eye pity-dim.
So fell a gentle rain on Manley's cheeks,
Out of the tender blue of his own eyes.
"Dear, little brother, tell me why you weep."
"You are so kind you hurt me, Magia."
"I would not hurt you, not for all the world."
"I know it, Magia, but you do forget
That brave hearts find it sweeter to give help
Than to receive it. Always being helped,
And never helping, makes a brave heart sick."
"Dear brother, they who love well never know
How much or in what ways they help, because
By nature, as our breathing, it is done."
But Magia saw he was not comforted.

They found that day a place called "Little Hell"
By the poor slaves who toiled there through long
   hours
Beneath the unlashed eyeball of the sun.
Here Magia restrained her heart and hands
From offices of love: "I have been dull,"
She whispered to her heart, "not to have seen
That even kindness sometimes has a sting."
Now when the summer sat upon her throne,

Mantled in dust and fire, and the blue sky
Was like a furnace roof, and the blue lake
Was like a furnace floor from which hot blasts
Were belched into the city, came a day
When little Manley wilted like a flower,
And white and gasping fell upon the floor,
And the command was given to bear him off
And lay him on a heap of dirty rags
Behind a door that shut off any breath
Of languid air that might have chanced to breathe
Across his forehead. Magia, at her work,
Heard something of the momentary stir,
And turning, missed her brother from his place.
She fled away to seek him. Bending low,
She bathed his face with water from a cup
And tears from her full eyelids: "Brother, wake!
Why do you sleep so strangely? Brother, wake!"
And presently, as when a light wind stirs
Between the leaves of a white rose, his lids
Quivered and parted, and his pale lips smiled:
"I've only earned a dollar every week.
How weak I am to faint and earn but that!"
"Why, Manley, I have never earned but two,
But there's no need of buying coal, you know;
God keeps up such hot fires in the sun,
And we can make three dollars last a week."
"Here, damn you! get to work! It's bad enough
To have one bag of bones upon the floor,"
Roared like the wind a voice in Magia's ear.
A pair of lurid eyeballs glared on her.
The brave child Magia simply answered him:

"I will not leave my brother; he is sick.
You are the cruelest man in all the world."
"Take the sick kitten home and nurse him there,
And see you do not bring him here again."
"O Magia, how strong and brave you are!"
Spoke Manley, leaning sweetly on her arm,
For brave hearts sometimes find it sweet to lean.
"I've read in books and sometimes heard men say
That girls are weak and timid, but I think
That when God tries to make a woman brave,
She has an angel courage that outdares
The noisy valor and brute force of men."
Spoke Magia softly, "Yes, I know men say
That girls are weak and fearful, but somehow
I think we're made of the same stuff as men.
What is there noble that a man dare do,
I dare not do, if there be need of it?
I am afraid of nothing in the world,
Except of being ungenerous or unkind,
Or doing anything which is untrue."
And so they talked together as they took,
Seeking the shadows, their slow homeward way.

Now brought the peaceful autumn sunnier days
Unto the little slaves. They having found
A kinder master, and being older grown,
Performed their work with more efficient hands,
And wiser heads by harsh experience trained.
And Magia grew and blossomed day by day,
As lithe and strong and slender as a plant
That has sweet tutelage of sun and wind,

All gentle ministry of rain and dew,
And the rich sustenance of fertile soil;
And Manley, growing too, though slowlier,
Increased in stature and in thews of limb,
And on his cheek there came a faltering flush.
According as the body slowly grows,
Ofttimes the soul grows fast, too strong and fast.
Years make not old, but sorrow; one night's frost,
And lo! the delicate bloom of youth is gone.
So grew the soul of Manley strong and fast.
He thought as men do, felt as men do, lived
In fifteen years as much as most men do
In twice fifteen. And strangely stirred his blood,
As the deep mysteries of human life
Broke on his dazzled being, and his heart
Began to start and flutter at the touch
Of Magia's hand, the music of her voice.
Her grace was in the motion of the trees,
Her laughter in the rippling of the waves,
Her smile gleamed in the starlight, and he said,
"I will not call her 'sister' by and by,
But only 'Magia,' and then—and then—
I'll call her 'sweetheart,' oh! and then—and then—
I'll call her 'wife.'" And so he dreamed a dream,
And lived in it until the present grew
Misty and dim about him. Many souls
Thus live in moonlight, melancholy, sweet,
Of a to-morrow that is ever lit
By the reflected light of some bright orb
Of unseen happiness that shines afar.
Love is a bird that comes to every heart,

Each in its season, to some soon, some late,
To wake the deep recesses with its thrills
Of tuneful song, to stir the yet green leaves
Of promise, gather up the scattered shreds
Of faded joys and tufts of soft dream-down
From long-forsaken pillows, bear them up
Into the sunlight, and green boughs of hope,
To build of them a nest in which to brood
The snowy dream-eggs of new life and song.
So early came the bird to Manley's heart,
Filling its depths with melody; the while
Dwelt Magia in the sunlight of to-day,
In childhood's slumberous, sweet unconsciousness
Of pain and passion. And so flowed the years,
Another and another and another,
Until it seemed that they would flow on so
Forever and forever and forever.

But down the aisle one morning passed a youth,
Giving command on either hand like one
Clothed with authority. His curls were brown
As the ripe nuts of autumn, and his eyes
Of one tint with his curls. His lips were red
As ripe twin berries, lithe his form and straight,
And eloquent with motion, and his smile
Was such a one as being meant for none,
Yet seemed bestowed on each particular face
With an especial sweetness. So he passed
Smiling on all wan faces, till he came
To Magia's counter, where he paused and gazed,
Then passed on, muttering beneath his breath,

"By Jove, the prettiest face I ever saw!"
Upon the morrow morn he came and talked
About the pretty laces that she sold,
And said, "I think you have not slaved long thus
For little, in a dark and dingy place."
And Magia answered, smiling, "Five years, sir!"
"By Jove! I think those roses that you wear
The hardiest ever bloomed on maiden's cheek."
Each day he stood by Magia and leaned
His face down smiling, till the whisper ran,
"He has a lover's look for Magia."
And once he gently took her hand in his;
Her face was lifted glowing like a flower
On which a sudden gleam of sunlight falls.
She said within herself, "He likes me well,
And I am glad. 'Twas never so before.
It will be better for my brother now."
Late on an afternoon he passed and said
In a low, sudden whisper, bending down
Until his red lips seemed to touch her curls,
"Your books are wrong. Come back a little while
After the rest are gone, past six o'clock,
And I will show you where the error is."
So Magia, mutely wondering, took her way
Along the crowded highway to the bridge,
Then, smiling, turned, "My brother, do not wait,
For Mr. Grandville says my books are wrong,
And bids me come to have them straightened out."
He answered nothing, but the hot blood burned
Away the spirit whiteness of his brow.
He stood and leaned and watched a stately boat

Puffing its slow way through the yawning bridge,
And pressed his hands together. Magia passed
Within the door, and stood to wait the will
Of him who bade her thither. When he came,
He swung the heavy door upon its hinge,
And turned the heavy key within its lock,
Then set his back against the door, meanwhile
Crossing his youthful arms and looked at her;
And in his look was something new and strange.
Something which burned and blighted, clothed her
    cheek
With blushes for a shame which was not hers,
A shame she understood not—blushes pure
For man's impurity, discerned afar
And faintly in the pure depths of her soul—
Far off like smoke in an unclouded heaven;
And like some flowers by nature sweetly taught
To fold themselves away from human touch,
She gathered up herself into herself,
And with a shiver shut her eyelids down.
He said, "Your books are wrong, but there's a way
To set them right. I've helped the girls before."
Quickly the cherub innocence in her
Grew to a wise archangel, armed and strong.
She raised her fearless eyes and looked at him,
As if she looked upon a loathsome worm
That crawled upon a white fold of her dress,
And which she brushed off with a shuddering touch,
A shudder born of loathing and not fear;
And then she lifted up her little hand
With an imperious gesture, and he shrank

And cowered, and again she raised her hand
With that imperious gesture, and he moved,
And like a serpent by an angel's eye
Charmed to her will, wide open set the door,
And stood aside, with eyes cast meekly down
In gentle reverence, to let her pass.

All night upon her pillow Magia tossed,
And reasoned with herself what course were wise.
"For if I go, my brother will go too,
And there's no likelihood that we can find
Another place so suited to his strength.
But if I stay and keep as still and pure
As snow upon a hidden mountain ledge,
What harm can come to me or any one?"

Upon the morrow morn a better place
Was made for Manley with increase of pay,
And Arthur Grandville, passing Magia's way,
Scarce looked at her, or if perchance he spoke
On necessary business, then his tone
Was low and full of gentle reverence.
But Manley's face was overcast with gloom.
And Magia said, "What is it I have done?
I have been over anxious to be kind,
Have helped him sometimes when there was no need
Forgetting kindness sometimes has a sting.
I will be wise and watchful after this."
So she restrained herself from helpful deeds
That were so natural, and asked instead,
"My brother, kindly bring me this, or that;"

Or, "Brother Manley, help me with this task
I pray;" or, "Please to carry this for me."
Whereat he always flashed into a smile.
Once Magia came and laid a loving hand
On either shoulder, as she sometimes did,
And leaned her lips to his, her rich, warm lips.
The conscious color leaped into his cheeks;
He pushed her gently from him: "You forget
That you are not my sister, Magia;
There is no tie of blood between us two."
She started back in pale, large-eyed surprise:
"Ah! brother Manley, you forget that I
First taught you the sweet lesson of a kiss."
"Nay, Magia, I remember it so well
That it reminds me that there is no tie
Of blood between us two." She answered him
With lips that quivered, and with hands hard
    clasped,
"Oh! there are sometimes gulfs as deep as hell
Between hearts bound as close as blood can bind,
While others, fettered by no natural ties,
Move side by side together through the world,
As we may often see two stars in heaven,
Bound by no visible cord, yet wandering on,
Brother and sister-like among the spheres.
Oh! kiss me, Manley; be my brother still!"
He leaned and kissed her then, and went away,
And laid himself upon the cool white sand,
And turned his pale face toward the cool green sea.
"Mad, foolish thought within a mad fool's brain—
To dream that I could be a mate for her!

I dreamed and waked not until yester morn,
When by an accident I saw us three
Reflected in a mirror. Did I say,
'An accident it seemed?' and yet it seemed
As if the hands of doom and destiny
Were laid upon my brow to make me turn
And look upon the vision. There we stood,
They two together with their curls flung back.
Their cheeks were ripe with youth, and he so strong
And tall and lithe and bright and beautiful,
And she more bright and beautiful than he.
I stood apart so small and sad and pale,
With stooping shoulders and with slender limbs.
I saw the vision, and my heart leaped up,
I almost heard it cry out in my breast.
But I will love her still, and love her well,
As loves the sea the moon—far off, far off,
And follows her forever 'round the world,
Crowning itself with jewels in her light,
Reflecting all her phases—for I know
I shall be nobler loving one so pure;
And then—and then—love is not all of life.
I shall grow learned and good and wise and strong,
Winning an angel mastery o'er myself,
And do perhaps some great work in the world,
And men shall say, 'How good is it he lived!'"

The white moon like a fair young shepherdess,
Above him watched amid her starry flock,
Feeding on light as they moved tranquilly
Through the wide, dewy pastures of the skies.

He rose and walked across the cool, white sands,
And turned into the street that homeward led.

> NOTE: I am indebted to a series of articles in the *Times* for 1888, for some of the incidents in Part II of this book.—THE AUTHOR

PART III

REVOLT

"Sweet sister, let us rest upon our oars.
The evening flings his purple mantle wide,
And shows his starry girdle. Tell me, pray,
How many do you love in all the world?"
"My mother and my brother."
                                      "None but these?"
"None other; I have no one else to love."
"And do you love me truly, Magia?"
"Whom should I love, my brother, if not you?
Who is so kind to me in all the world?"
"We do not always love those hearts the best
That beat most kindly toward us, and God knows
We cannot help it. Hearts are curious things.
But, sister, there's a thing that I would say.
I have not been a spy upon your ways,
But a fond brother's eyes are quick to see
What threats a sister's happiness, and I
Have marked how often Grandville takes your hand!
How low and tenderly he speaks to you!
And you are kind to him. I like it not,
Because I like him not; he is not true.

I speak with reason; trust me, Magia."
"If he but knew it is for love of him
That I am kind for most part—but no, no!
I would not have him know for all the world,
For all the world and all the stars in heaven."
So Magia spoke in silence with herself,
And then aloud: "But surely it is good
To treat the sins of men with gentleness,
As you would treat a sickness of the flesh,—
For are they not a sickness of the soul?—
And heal them with the touch of purity
And truth and honor!"
     "Sister Magia,
I oft have seen the black filth of the street
Smirch up the angel whiteness of the snow,
But I have never seen the purest snow
Convert the slime and vileness of the street
Into a snowy whiteness."
     "But he's kind.
Shall kindness, brother, not be kindly met?"
"I say there is no honor in the world
That is not tarnished by expediency.
I say there is no kindness in the world
That does not bear the rust of selfishness.
To do the kindly act where lies the need,
In the first pure, virgin impulse of the heart,
Stead of where lies the earnest of reward,
Demands such calm, unbiased heights of love,
Sweet courage and brave purpose—heights so far
Above the common levels of the world
That few have ever gained their starry peace.

Do not our laws confess that men are brutes,
Incapable of noble self-restraint,
By licensing the brutish and the base
In human nature, making our great sins
Simply a little costlier than our less?
None is for the sweet sake of goodness, good,
Gaining an angel mastery of himself,
Without the fear of evil or the hope
Of profit."

"True, my brother, true, and yet,
Had all the angels sinned with Lucifer,
But one being leal and steadfast unto God,
By him is angelship made possible
In heaven forever, to angels after-born,
Redeeming angelhood. So Christ, being pure,
Made purity ever possible to men,
Redeeming mankind. Brother, it is true
That Circe boldly walks amid the throng,
And builds her palaces on every street,
Inviting men to enter and be swine,
And most men without blushing enter in.
But since I know my brother is heart-pure,
Untarnished by the baseness of the world,
Through him my heart will keep its faith in man."
He turned and looked upon her with a smile:
"Faith!—faith in God, that is, in ultimate good,
Faith in humanity, in thine own soul—
Of all the virtues faith's the fairest star
Of those that 'round the splendor of the soul,
Cluster and show its brightness, like the sun
Clasped by his shining rosary of worlds.

Do you believe in me, my sister?"

"Yes."

"And in no other man?"

"None other."

"Thanks!
That is the sweetest tonic of my life."
Then they took up their oars, and silence reigned,
Except the silver clash of oar and wave,
And the soft kissing of the liquid lips
Of sleepless waters on the little skiff,
While many rays of starshine, softly blent,
Made a faint splendor, till the rising moon
Flung out a silver plank across the sea,
Like a fair ship unto her moorings come.
Then slowly shoreward moved the little boat,
And the sweet Sabbath rest was at an end.
Then after three nights Arthur Grandville came,
In all the fair assurance of bright youth,
And sat at Magia's feet, and bowed his head
Above her hands, and murmured, "Magia,
You are the sweet saint whose rebuking smile
Has curbed the youthful passion of my blood,
And waked the angel yearning in my breast
To stand beside you, pure as you, nay, more—
For he who once has tasted sin, and been
A slave to passion and to appetite,
Then throttled both, and stood up brave and strong
And angel-pure, is more than angels are,
Who never have been tempted, nor have known
The witchery of passion. O beloved,
I never knew how lovely virtue was,

How beautiful are purity and truth,
What joy to make our strongest passions slaves,
And lead them captive at the chariot wheels
Of some pure, conquering purpose, until you
Unveiled the mystic beauty unto me.
Deal kindly with me; I was never taught
That license is not liberty, nor yet,
By kindly circumstances nobly wrought.
For what we are, we are, not of ourselves,
But from the hissing crucible of life,
Poured out into the iron mold of things,
Stamped with the universe that is and was,
And all the long, long æons. Magia,
Will you not come and help me to be good?"
"Sir, I can never love you, though I fain
Would help you to be pure. Pray loose my hands.
I cannot love you, and I pray you go."
"You shall not send me from you, Magia.
No, for your brother's sake you *will* not. Know
His comfort and promotion are with me."
"Is this the newly wakened angel's voice?"
Was Magia's low and sorrowful response.
"It is an infant angel, and its voice
Is but a plaintive, inarticulate cry.
It must be watched and nurtured tenderly."
"Sir, you are young and strong and beautiful;
Is there no other one to love you well?"
"There is a fair, sweet girl, with locks like rays
Of golden light about the brow of morn,
And she has loved me long and loved me well.
But if I love her not, what then, what then?"

"I think we are too apt to lightly prize
Affections easily and always ours."
"You will not send me from you, Magia,
And strangle the new yearning in my breast?
You will be kind at least, and grant to me
One touch of your pure lips upon my own,
To be the inspiration of new hopes.
You would not feel its loss more than the sun
Would miss a little sunbeam going forth,
Laden with life for some despairing flower."
Then Magia wavered, arguing with herself,
"If I could do him good, and so bring good
Unto my brother, should I not do this?"
She said, "For his sake and for yours!" then stooped
And gently kissed him, and the little clock
Upon the mantel, sharp and shrill, struck nine;
And Manley passed before the open door,
Unseen, but seeing with wide, glittering eyes.
He fled into the night and seized a boat
And bending all his strength, rowed fast and far
Beyond the bar, then laid aside his oars,
And listened to the chuckling of the waves
That seemed to mock his sorrow, and he cried:
"I think, if death had taken her in his arms,
And kissed the mirth and music from her lips,
I think I could have kissed her eyelids then,
And her lips' richness with the rose-mist gone,
And her brow's marble with the thought-grace fled
The cold snow of her throat, her cheeks, her hands,
And whispered, 'O belovèd, thou art missed,
But still thy memory lingers like a glow,

An after-sunset splendor that will bridge
The darkness 'twixt the evening and the dawn
Of parting and of meeting. But to know
That she has stooped to baseness; that she is
Less noble than I thought her; that her heart
Is not the pure and perfect pearl I thought
Beat in her bosom, this is agony,
A thorn to which the mighty sting of death
Is as a tender rose. My heart, my heart,
How thou dost ache, being full of frozen tears,
Which yet will burst thee if thou dost not ease
Thyself by weeping or by utterance!
Have I not oft read poems quivering
With lovers' heart-beats, written to allay
Their secret heart-pain? I will write one too:

"'Twas not you that I loved, but an ideal that grew
   in my brain,
Like a beautiful infant angel unconscious of pain,
Born of my heart and my brain, and nursed to its fill
At the rose-tinged, white bosom of Fancy through
   long months, until
It stood up beautiful, strong, full-statured, complete
From radiant wing-tip to wing-tip, white forehead
   to feet.
Then I searched till I found a woman's fair form to
   enshrine
Most fitly my angel, then cried, 'Thou art mine!
   thou art mine!'
Then I knelt, and I worshiped, and wept in a trans-
   port of bliss,
Till a voice, through the shock of events, cried
   aloud, 'What is this?
Look, fool!' And I saw that the shrine had been
   fractured; and lo,

Through the flaw all the want and the weakness
  were visible. Oh!
In anguish I learned that my shrine was not fit to
  retain
My beautiful ideal; that I must receive it again.
If an angel leaned over the golden edge of yon star,
And motioned the spheres into silence, and whis-
  pered from far
That the music and splendor of heaven would make
  full amend
For the discord and darkness of earth from begin-
  ning to end,
I think I should dare then to challenge his angelic
  word;
I should laugh as I answered, "Thou snow-plumed,
  heavenly bird,
Escaped from God's palm trees of peace! O thou
  star-crested dove,
What knowest thou of the human passion of love,
With its thrills and its anguish? Return to thy
  bowers of bliss.
All heaven can never atone for an hour like this.'"

This does not ease my heartache. Oh! I would
That I could take up some sweet instrument,
And breathe myself out through its trembling strings!
For music is the language of those deep
Emotions that, too subtle even for thought,
Burst from the heart in sweet concordant sounds,
Breathing the yearning passion and the pain
That human speech is impotent to bear.
God, if thou hast an angel yet to spare,
Send him to comfort me. How vain I speak!
For prayer is but man's low wail of despair,
His infant cry of weakness, his complaint
Against the might and majesty of things.

Lo, when I pray, see how the words drop back
Upon my burning heart, like meteors
Cast upward from the sun, to fall again
Into its seething bosom, or go forth
Into the darkness, and sink cold and dead.
Listen, my heart, thou never wilt grow strong,
Till thou hast learned to battle, and not cry,
'Help, help!' for there is none to give thee help.
Each thrids his night of agony alone,
Feels out sometimes to find a strong, bright soul
To lean on, thinks he finds one, tries to lean.
Alas! it fails him where he needs it most.
He learns 'tis easier to move upright,
Self-poised, self-balanced like a wheeling star
About his own soul's center. Magia,
O Magia, do I not love thee still?
Can I forget all in one little hour,
Thy gentle tones, the sweet wine of thy lips,
And the perpetual daybreak on thy brow,
Thy gracious readiness to kindly deeds—
Things woven into the tissues of my soul
By years of tender intercourse? No, no!
I must unravel through slow months and years,
This shining thread from out the warp and woof
Of all my being, loving somewhat still.
Now will I hold myself aloof from men,
With just enough of contact to preserve
A kindly human warmth about the heart,
And make myself a world of love and truth,
Honor and purity, with noble thoughts,
And the great, gracious souls that dwell in books.

I will not be a hermit, for I know
The world needs every pure life. A true man
Should have an upward and a downward reach,
One hand grip earth, the other grasp at heaven.
I never thought much of Saint Simeon,
Who let the pure life in him run to waste
On a grim pillar, cheating men of good."
So Manley, moving homeward, mused, and so,
Flushed with fresh resolution like new wine,
His heart beat lighter, and his lips half smiled
As Magia met him: "Brother, why so late?"
"My sister, wherefore do you wait for me?"
"Wherefore? and wherefore not, since you are sad?
Tell me your trouble; I will comfort you."
"Some sorrows, sister, must be borne alone."
"But there are heavy rings around your eyes.
You used not thus to talk, but ever spoke
Your griefs and troubles freely in my ear."
"Yes, children prattle, and I was a child.
If I feel strong, shall I make boast of it?
A boast is hateful in the sight of heaven;
For, mark you, when you boast that anything
Is thus, or thus, according to your wish
The contrary will happen. If I say
'I have not slipped in this way for thus long,'
'I'm doubtless cured of this fault,' straight I slip;
Or if I say, 'This pain is vanquished quite,'
Straightway the dead nerve twinges, and I think
That silence is the badge of dignity.
In youth mind's golden center lieth bare,
But ripening years do shrine it in like leaves,

Because we learn that there is none to help."
"God help you, brother, if I cannot."
                                    "No,
God cannot help me; I must help myself.
For there is a divinity within,
A spirit and a power that compels
Us on and on to shape our destiny;
To wrestle godlike with the iron bands
Of social wrong, and of inevitable,
Cold, blind necessity of natural laws,
That, riveted upon the rocks of time,
Would hold us down forever and forever,
The while above us, upon eagle wings,
Our aspirations, hovering, ascend
And descend, feeding on our beating hearts."
Then Magia clasped her hands upon her brow,
And answered very slowly, reverently:
"I know not if there be what men call God,
A power divine, external to ourselves,
That guides the arm of Justice when she strikes,
And through the vast unmeaning of men's ways
Weaves out sublimest purpose; but somehow,
There is an inward faith, a conscious rest
On something constant in the whirl of change,
A power divine that makes the right to win,
And on the beautiful feet of goodness, swift
And sure, makes good to follow." Magia paused,
And Manley turned the sorrow of his eyes
Upon the eager beauty of her face:
"Each act of ours will have its sure result.
Deceive, and you will have deception's fruits.

Be sure no angel stands behind our deeds
To gather up the tangled ends we leave,
And weave them into beautiful designs.
And what we are, we are because we will.
The stern, invincible rocks of circumstance,
Formed by the ages that have gone before,
'Gainst which we beat ourselves like ocean waves,
Make the bright foam and music of our lives.
A splendid anvil is necessity,
On which we lay our souls like glowing steel,
And with the mighty hammer of the will,
Amid the ringing notes and flying sparks,
Beat out that which we are and will to be."
"You seem so strange to-night you make me sad.
I do not understand you, but I think
It is the strange books that you read of late.
Tell me their names, and I will read them too,
So comprehend you."
     "'Tis not what we know,
Nor yet what we believe, but what we are
That fashions our Hereafter, as our Here.
Be true, whatever else you are, be true."
"Why talk to me, my brother, of deceit,
And being true? Am I not always true?"
"My sister, you are always kind."
        "Not kind
But true, say true."
      "My sister, always kind!"
With that he turned and kissed her and went out.
But Magia sat still with chin on hand,
With eyelids drooping, and with tremulous mouth:

"The night is close, and I am sad at heart.
How is it I have so offended him?
Perhaps I am too loving for a girl
That is no kin of his.   He thinks me bold,
Wanting somewhat in maidenly reserve.
How can I learn to blush beneath his glance,
I who have looked so frankly in his eyes,
As if he were my brother, all these years?
True, we were children, and, dear God, I would
We could be always children, simple, pure,
As frank and free and fond as children are.
Hereafter I will teach myself reserve
And all restraint becoming to a girl
Who is no kin of his."   And so it was
That Magia met her brother with a smile
That was like frost upon a sunny morn—
Bright and yet cold, and all her words and ways
Were gentle but restrained, and still they went
Together to their work and home again,
And Manley's heart ached hard against his will,
Seeing how cold and distant she had grown.
Magia gathered up his every word,
And analyzed it in her secret soul.
Was heaven wise to lock each human heart.
With such a mystic spring that but one key,
Which heaven itself may never duplicate,
And but the owner in the lock may turn,
Will bid it open?   Were it otherwise,
The lover, yearning in his heart to know
The heart of his belovèd, might sometimes
Set soft the door ajar, and see her there,

Who with a calm word and indifferent smile,
Late met him coldly—see her bending low
Above the heaped up treasures of his smiles
And tender words and glances. "Ah!" she says,
"How tender is this smile! This one how bright!
This tremulous with fear, this touched with pain!
This jeweled word will match the tender smile;
See how it glistens with half-uttered thought!
And this one hath a subtle meaning in it;
And this one hath the ruddy glow of hope;
And this one hath a dark and anxious gleam.
I'll string them all upon a single thread,
And see what beauty and what grace they have,
When linked together." And so Magia,
Locked in herself, communing with herself,
Reviewing Manley's words and ways, confessed,
"I love him, though I know not how I love—
'As sweetheart or as sister or as friend.
I do not understand love, but I know,
If loving means to be most sad at heart,
Whenever from the heart, like a pale mist,
A cloud of doubt floats up between us two,
And hides us from each other; if to love,
Means to be happy only in his smile,
And seeking for his good—why then, I love."
So was it Manley, locked within himself,
Reviewing Magia's words and ways, confessed,
"I love her still, whatever she has done.
Whatever she has done, she meant no wrong.
I understand what love is, and I know,
If loving is to trust the one beloved

Against the witness of the eye and ear,
To find the sweetest pleasure in her smile,
And seeking for her good—why then, I love.
She said she loved but two in all the world,
And if she said it, it was wholly true,
Whatever act of hers gainsay her words,
For by no act meant she to be untrue.
I know there is no evil in her heart,
For there's an atmosphere in which we float,
Like stars in ether, breathed out of the soul,
A spiritual ether, and all they
Who come into our presence, breathing it,
May surely tell if we be true or false."
So Manley went to Magia with a smile
As frank and sweet as when he was a child:
"Forgive me; I was sad the other night,
And all the world seemed muffled in a cloud.
Forgive me, Magia, be my sister still,
And I will be your brother as we were
In the sweet days of childhood." Magia sprang
And twined her arms about his neck and cried,
"And we shall love as children once again."

That was at early morning, and the sun
Kissed their fair foreheads as their young lips met.
At evening Arthur Grandville came again,
And Manley calmly rose and yielded up
His place at Magia's side, and quit the room.
Then Arthur tossed the rich locks from his brow,
And turned the passionate bloom of his young face
Toward Magia, smiling: "What a world is this!

A marvelous world to him whose veins are full
Of the bright streams of youthfulness and strength,
When life is wooing him at every sense,
And every sense, wide open like a flower,
Is drinking life in;—then if the warm beam
Of ripening love should fall upon that life,
How rich and sweet it grows! O Magia,
If love begetteth love, as I am told,
Then I shall win your love by strength of mine."
He caught her in his arms and held her fast,
And Magia, struggling faintly, sick at heart,
Fearful lest any one should hear a sound,
Murmured through tremulous white lips, "Set me free,
Or I shall surely hate you! Set me free!"
At that he loosed his clasp, and Magia sprang,
All crimson as the sunrise with the shame
And anger of her spirit: "Pray you, go.
To morrow we will find another place.
I will not, even for my brother's sake,
Bear with you longer. It would grieve his heart.
I wrong him by my kindness; that's not kind."
"No, Magia, you will not go away.
You shall have nothing more to bear from me,
And I will take no worse revenge than this,
To treat your brother kindlier than before.
You will not send me from you, Magia,
And strangle those new yearnings in my heart,
Toward purity and goodness?"
       Manley sat
Within his chamber, wrestling with himself,

Like Jacob with the angel: "Shall I steal,
And look upon her through the open door,
See if her face be tender, kind or cold?
No, I will not distrust her by a look;
For if all evidence proclaimed her false,
Against the witnessing of every sense
I should believe her true. And yet—and yet—
Thou shiningest archangel, strong enough
To stand unveiled the nearest to the throne
Of the Eternal One, beware, boast not
Thy power to resist and pass unscathed
All earth's temptations. There is none that knows,
Till tempted, what temptation is—its power
To paralyze the will and steep the brain
In deep forgetfulness; but he who once
Has stood on ruin's brink with fainting heart
And reeling brain, with pleading hands and eyes
Uplifted to the stars, deals evermore,
Gently with those that err. I do believe
That he who highest climbs above the brute,
Closest to angelhood, being finer wrought,
Is tempted more and more, and suffers more
Through wrestling with temptation, by response
To subtleties of passion and of pain,
That grosser natures never feel."
                                        He rose,
And then, as if a magnet drew him on,
He crept along the dark and narrow hall
To where the lamplight glimmered through the
    door.
He saw the rosy light on Grandville's face.

Bent over Magia's, hidden on his breast.
Their rich curls flowed together, and their tones
Were low and passionate. Then Manley's heart
Gave a great throb of doom, and his brain swam.
Forward into the shadow, on his face,
He fell, his hands locked tight, until the nails
Wounded the fair flesh. Every now and then,
He whispered in the darkness, "I believe,
Yes, I believe, I do believe in her."
He rose up presently and groped his way
Down the dark, narrow stairs, and through the door
Into the gaslight, when an arm was linked
Through his in friendly way, and Grandville said,
With kind, familiar grace, as was his way:
"Come, let us stroll together toward the lake.
The night is close; perhaps the languid wind
Is stirring weary wings about the shore.
Besides, I needs must have a word with you."
"About my sister?"
                      "Ah! how well you guess!"
"Because it is the finest strings respond
To lightest touches, and the finest string
That vibrates in my heart, is love of her."
"You cannot blame me then for loving too?"
"If I can blame the flowers for loving light!"
"And if the light should deign to love a flower,
You would not blame it?"
                    "But the light, you know,
Love's weeds and flowers and all that is, alike,
And makes itself no darlings in the world."
"We'll leave the fancy then, of light and flowers.

Tell me, would you be glad or sorrowful
To know that Magia loved me?"   Manley smiled,
Faintly at first like the pale streak of dawn
That brighter grows and brighter till the east
Is glorious and glowing with the flush
Expectant of the sunrise; so his smile
Kindled from lip to cheek, from cheek to brow,
And in his heart he answered ere his lips
Could shape the words of a steadfast reply:
"Oh! you unsheathe a sword against my breast,
And like a noble Roman, fearing shame,
The shame of being conquered by the strength
Of mine own weakness, I will fall on it,
And pierce my young heart through, and then arise
Out of the blood and anguish, and exclaim,
'How well I died!'"   And then he spoke aloud:
"We seek the happiness of those we love.
If loving you will make her sweet soul glad,
I shall be glad too."
                    "Ah! you are indeed
A fond and faithful brother.   One thing more—
Will you not tell her this?   One word of yours
Will have more weight to tip the scale with her
Than all my pleading, for she loves you well.
Nay, were you not her brother, I should feel
The ache of jealousy because of you.
Are we not well matched, being both young and
    strong,
And nature having given to us both
The gift of human beauty—a rich gift
To those who wear it graciously and feel

No arrogance because of it; and then
I have an ample fortune for us both.
Are we not well matched?"
      "Aye, you are indeed."
"Then will you speak to her in my behalf,
Urging her gently for my sake?"
         "I will."
"Thanks! thanks! You are my brother now indeed,
A noble fellow! Now, good night!"
        "Good night!"
Then Grandville, turning south, went cityward,
While Manley northward moved along the shore,
Until he found a stretch of sandy beach,
Where gurgling through the stones, the water crept
With the soft sound of kissing. There he knelt,
His face turned toward the gray, complaining sea:
"Tell thyself truth, my heart, they are well matched,
For he is bright and beautiful like her,
And all the evil thoughts I had of him,
Were but a prejudice of my own mind,
Born of a selfish dread of losing her.
I will break every chain that binds my soul
From doing justice. Yes, I will be free.
However much a slave to other men,
I will not be in bondage to myself.
What art thou, Liberty, sweet Liberty?
Art thou in broken bars and rended chains,
In shattered thrones and trampled codes, blood-writ,
In strangled trusts that erst had tyrannized
Over earth's trade and commerce and man's bread,
In laws repealed, emancipation acts,

Dead institutions that outlived their use,
Disabled great political machines,
The right to equal shares of light and air
And standing room upon this ample star,
The right to have the fruits of one's own toil;—
Art thou in these things, O sweet Liberty?
Thy breath is in them all, but thou art not.
Oh! liberty is the grand consciousness
Of strength to sever every cord that draws
The soul away from its sublimest course
Of perfect truth and honor to itself—
The slender silken cord of gratitude,
So soft, and yet as strong as fine-wrought steel—
That stronger chain whose shining golden links
Are obligations wrought out of good turns,
Each heavily conditioned like a bond,
Expressly or impliedly, that it bring
Each turn a full return or forfeiture
Of all the doer's further acts of grace—
The strong steel bands opinions lay on us,
Strongest by those we love. Such chains as these
Are subtly woven around us day by day.
Oh! we are free if strong enough to rise,
And, with that brightest, bravest sword of man—
The will to do or not to do the thing
Himself deems right or wrong unto himself,
To sever every fetter laid on us
By law or love or custom, unsustained
By justice, truth and reason. Once again,
I will be lord and master of myself.
I will arise and go to Magia."

Thrice he arose and moved a little way,
And thrice he turned again and stretched his hands
Toward the gray waters, while his pale lips moved,
But spoke no audible word and breathed no sigh.
O heart of love and longing, what art thou?
Dost count for nothing in the vast of things?
In thee what storms rage, and what fair stars rise!
Angels take counsel in thee, and fiends lurk,
And sometimes heaven reigns, and sometimes hell;
Yet no one passing even hears thee beat.
For nothing? Aye, for something:—some one writes
How once an empire fell. The world says, "Ah!"
And never pausing, goes about its work.
There comes a poet with a tuneful tongue,
And sings about the breaking of a heart
That's mixed with heart-dust for a thousand years;
And lo, the world is melted into tears.

Meanwhile, beside her white unrumpled couch
Knelt Magia, all her dark curls drenched with tears:
"Oh! to be free, free, free—free to be true
Unto myself, to shun whom I would shun,
To love whom I would love, and free to say,
'O my beloved, I love you,' without shame.
For if we love, why not act lovingly,
Speak lovingly, because we can but read
And judge each other by the outward signs.
God does not send an angel forth from heaven
To gather up our thistles from the wind,
And change them into roses for our feet.
Oh! I am but a slave; I dare not act

My will for fear of harm." Sweet Magia,
Thou dost but swell the universal moan
Of human slavery, but iterate
The universal cry for freedom. Lo,
This wondrous social fabric we have woven,
Majestic in proportions, in design
So intricate that all the world cries out,
"A master product of the human brain!"
Is a vast web, a snare, imprisoning
The beautiful and valiant in man's life,
Like jealous Vulcan's fine-wrought golden snare.
And underneath the fair externe, i' th' dark
Of the sub-structure, lies a mesh of chains,
Heavy and cold and rusted with men's tears.
With every throb of the great social heart,
Hark to the deadly rattle and the clank,
As they do bind and bruise and suffocate.

Hark!—some one lightly tapping: "Brother, come."
And Manley, entering, set himself a chair
Beside her where the moonlight softly shone,
Disputed by no artificial beam.
Then Magia flung her curls across his knees,
And hard against them pressed her tear-wet cheek.
He thrust his fingers in among her curls,
And felt their warmth and richness chilling him.
"How damp your cheek is with the summer heat!"
His presence brought her peace, and she was mute.
"How tenderly the moonbeams kiss your hair!"
"Why is it that the moonlight makes us sad?"
"Because 'tis a suggestion and a hint

Of far-off warmth and splendor we have not.
We're minded of the good that we have missed,
And sweet suggestions of life's grand Might Be
Fall on the soul like moonlight 'mid the hush
And cold and shadow of life's stern Must Be."
"You're sad to-night, my brother."
         "Only grave.
I walked with Grandville by the lake to-night.
He says he loves my sister. Is not this
Enough to make a loving brother grave?"
"And if I love him, will it make you glad?"
"Whatever gladdens you will gladden me.
I blame me that I ever spoke of him
With words of slur and slight, for now he seems
To have a manlier spirit than I thought,
And he is bright and beautiful like you.
I only nursed a foolish prejudice,
Born of a selfish dread of losing you."
"Have I not told you that I love but two,
My mother and my brother?"
        "So you have;
But do you know what re-creative force
Dwells in the little breast of one brief hour
To change us from the semblance of ourselves?
We sometimes face the image of ourselves
Of yesterday, that memory paints for us,
And start in wonder, asking, 'Is it I?'"
"I have not changed, my brother."
          "You are sure?"
 This moonlight is no surer." Then they sat
With the deep silence ringing in their ears,

And Manley felt an impulse in his soul
To speak himself out plainly, and to say,
"I am not bright and beautiful like you,
But I have strength of soul, and with my soul
I love you, my belovèd.   Answer me;
What is to be the tie between us two?"
And Magia felt a tremor in her blood.
A wild new thought was beating in her brain,
To dare to be herself, and to defy
The fiat of blind Custom, and to say,
"Dear brother Manley, you are my beloved.
If you are not my lover, I'll have none
In all the world, no, never in all the world.
What is to be the tie between us two?"
But still they heard the silence in their ears,
And neither dared to speak a word.   -
                                          Meanwhile
Amid his crimson cushions Grandville sat,
His rich brown curls piled up like autumn leaves
About his forehead's whiteness, and he smiled:
"There is no sweeter victory than this—
The conquest of a noble human heart;
And no defeat more full of pain than this—
To fail to win its favor.   I will win.
I have not been so good, nor yet so bad,
Considering I was never taught to draw
The rein upon my passions, nor deny
My senses any pleasure.   May the soul
Not bathe itself so oft in pure resolves,
And spread itself out to the gentle dews
Of holy inspirations, and absorb

The sweet sunlight of truth, till it is bleached
As snowy white as souls just from the loom
Of the Eternal Weaver, woven in tune
To the sweet symphonies of seraphim?
So will I cleanse my soul, and by her side,
Grow like her day by day and hour by hour,
As flowers that are planted side by side,
Borrow each other's tints. For Madeline,
My pretty Madeline, a face so fair
Wants not for worshipers."
       The changing leaves
Were falling fast where fell the kiss of death
On the ripe cheek of summer, on the day
When Magia and Manley, hand in hand,
As was their wont on sunny Sabbath days,
Roamed in the park together, while their feet
Trod rustling music from the dying leaves.
"Who is the stranger, Manley, who has come
To talk with you alone so oft of late?
And then so oft you sit and think and smile,
As if you had bright dreams, and I am glad."
He flushed a little as he answered her:
"Suppose that I were found to be sole heir
Of a rich uncle who had lately died
Intestate? Magia, what if 1 were rich?"
"I should be happy, Manley, for your sake."
He did not hear her answer, for his ears
Were deafened by the beating of his heart:
"This is the hour that I have dreamed upon.
This is the hour that I have lived so oft,
Rehearsing all its pulses ere it came.

This is the very moment." Then he spoke:
"There would be no more slavish toil for us.
We would be wholly free to follow out
The natural inclinations of our souls."
He paused to gather breath for that next word,
Whose wings should bear the spirit of his dreams,
And Magia took the pause to make reply:
"I've heard there is no thing in all the world
That is so potent to transform a man
As sudden wealth, but I presage no change
That will transform my brother from himself."
"No, Magia, all my riches would be yours,
And you should have all pleasure and all good
Earth could be bribed to give, and none should dare
To show you insult or indignity.
We would be slaves no more; we would be free."
"Dear brother, what is freedom? Tell me, pray,
If I must wait upon another's grace
To satisfy my needs, shall I be free?
I scarcely understand—I somehow think,
That love is best and sweetest that's most free.
Oh! I would rather love for love's own sake,
Unmixed with any dross of personal gain,
Save that large gain of soul that always comes
From loving any one that's pure and true.
I have no splendid gifts to cultivate,
And I am strong, and have no need of wealth;
But you, with all your noble gifts that want
Leisure for cultivation—you whose strength
Is not sufficient for the daily strain
Of unremitting toil, have need of wealth.

How happy I should be if you *were* rich!
But that would be a tale for fairy books.
For me I find much pleasure in the world.
Oh! there are drums and bugles in the sea,
And solemn organ thunders, and the wind
Plays upon flutes and trumpets, and the trees
Make of themselves sweet harps and violins.
I think there must be music everywhere,
If there is but a consonant chord in us,
And beauty, if our souls respond to beauty."
"Ah! Magia, there are worlds and worlds that lie
Beyond us that we dream not of until
We touch upon their shores, and catch, far off,
Sweet concord and bright visions unforedreamed.
We have no thirst or hunger for the things
That we have never tasted, but sometimes
A feverish craving for we know not what—
A blind, dumb passion feeling round the heart,
Unconscious of itself." But Magia smiled:
"I wish you wealth, my brother, but for me,
I am not ill content." Then Manley's heart
Fell in his bosom like a meteor
That, striking on the world's cold atmosphere,
Ceases to be a star and drops—a stone.
He found a deeper meaning in her words
Than Magia gave them, for his fine-strung soul
Vibrated, like a delicate instrument,
To imperceptible breathings of the wind.
A shadow fell before them in the sun,
And Arthur Grandville in their pathway stood,
And smiling stretched to either one a hand.

He said, "The autumn day is beautiful."
And Magia echoed faintly, "Beautiful!"
"Come, let us sit and rest a little while."
But Magia murmured, "No, I cannot sit.
I have already been too long from home;
But you, my brother, stay and rest a while,
So soft and pure the touches of the air."
Soon as her step had ceased to stir the leaves,
Then Grandville questioned with an eager smile:
"Did you present my cause? What did she say?"
"Nothing!"
   "What! nothing?"
       "No, not anything,
Though I did plead your case as best I could,
But this, 'I love but two in all the world,
My mother and my brother.'"
       "Pshaw! absurd!
Girls do not marry brothers."
      "Not of blood,
But there's no tie of blood between us two.
She found me when I was a feeble child
That knew not how to kiss, or even to smile;
That knew not what love meant; she found me then,
And taught me how to live, and ever since
Has called me brother. It is but a name."
"And do you say you are no kin to her?"
"None!"
   "None? Not a half-brother?"
       "No, not even
Step-brother!"
    "Well, what does she mean by this? —

To have you for a lover?"
"I know not,
But this I know, whatever she may mean,
That I do love her better than my life.
You think me not a fitting mate for her?"
"Well, to speak frankly, since you frankly ask,
When one is bright and beautiful like her,
One wishes her to wed with one as full
Of youthful strength and beauty, does he not?
Why do you grow so red and then so white?
I meant to speak but kindly, and indeed,
Your gentleness of manner, and the play
Of kindly thought upon your face, might well
Win such a gracious, tender soul as hers."
Then, faintly flushing, Manley slowly spoke:
"I came into possession recently
Of a fair fortune, and on yester eve
I made my will. I do not know what thought
Prompted me to it, but I made my will.
I laid it in a little secret drawer
To which this is the key; remember this."
"I'm glad of your good fortune," Grandville said.
"Our mutual love must make us mutual friends
Whatever be the outcome of it all.
At least we are too wise for enmity."
"Friends always, Grandville! See, the sun is low.
Our ways divide here."
"Well then, *friend*, good night!"
"Good night! I wish you well." Then Manley turned
And wandered north and eastward toward the lake,
And sat him down amid the withered leaves,

Beneath a rustling tree, and turned his face
Toward the blue lake, nor stirred for one long hour.
At last he drew a sheet of paper forth,
And laid it on his knee and slowly wrote,
Then folded it and waited till a child,
A little ragged boy, went strolling by,
Whistling a happy tune. To him he gave
The folded paper, bidding him to bear
It at the hour named, to whom he named,
And placed within the grimy little hand
So large and bright a guerdon that the boy
Whistled for joy and tossed his tattered cap,
And bounded lightly off. Then Manley turned
Himself again to silence and the sea,
Silence without, but tumult in his brain:
"Whenever I am weary of myself,
I know it is a sign of inward change,
A transformation working in my soul;
That soon or later I must cast aside
The withered semblance of my former self,
As sheds the locust its dry shell, and stand
A creature new and strange unto myself.
Shall I be conquered, I who oft have said,
'I will be lord and master of myself?'
The sin whose hideous face starts suddenly
Out of the darkness, makes us to recoil
With dread and horror, till we turn and fly;
But when we gaze upon it first far off,
And it approaches slowly, wooing us
With pleasant smiles and glances, till at last
Its hands clasp ours, its breath is on our cheeks,

Its kiss is on our lips, and its strong arms
Enfold us with a warm, magnetic clasp
That lulls to drowsiness all sense of wrong,
Then that which else were monstrous in our eyes,
Becomes a pleasant thing. I talk of sin;
Who says I sin if I shall take my life?
Is it not mine? Yet did I never ask
To have it given me, but it was thrust
Upon me, like a feeble, flickering flame.
Nor did I pray to keep it, but it burned
And burned on, till it grew too fierce and bright,
And now consumes me. Whose the right but mine
To bear the heat of this Promethean flame,
Or quench it in the blue lake, solving so,
Life's vain, insoluble problem easily?
I said I would create myself a world,
A world of spirits; others have done so,
And dwelt therein; but I—I want the flesh,
Rosy, warm flesh that I can find and fold.
Go, thou sweet wind, and kiss her fragrant curls,
Then come again, and wander through my locks!
Go thou, and move across her warm, red lips,
In whose sweet purity I have believed
Against the witnessing of every sense,
Then come again and bear that kiss to me.
My heart is breaking, Magia! 'Let it break!'
In laughter comes the mocking answer back
From the blue, leaping waves. The moon is risen.
The wind is blowing strongly from the west,
Piling the clouds up moonward, and the lake
Whitening with gathering passion frets and moans.

I think 'twill storm ere midnight. That is well."

Within her chamber meanwhile Magia stood,
Re-robing in a simple dress of white,
And rearranging the dark curls that twined
Vine-like about her temples, for the moon
Between the parted curtains softly beamed,
And lit up Magia's mirror where she stood,
Smiling upon the vision of herself.
"How fair I am! Yes, I am fair indeed.
How full and white the forehead flashes out
Of its dark curls! The eyes how luminous!
The lips how red! And see how gleams the throat!
How rare a gift is beauty rightly used!
Oh! he will be returning presently,
And I would rather *he* would think me fair—
That *he* would think me noble, brave and true,
Than any king that ever wore a crown.
I've dressed to night just as he likes me best.
I'll drape this lace across my bosom so.
That curl looks better this way. See, my cheek
Is clothed with burning blushes, for a thought
Has ripened to a purpose in my brain,
And will this night be born a perfect act.
See how my cheek glows redder with the shame
Of such presumptuous thoughts, and yet I think
He magnifies his frailty, and I think—
I'll think the thought so softly in my brain,
The beating of my heart shall drown it. Yes,
I think he thinks—I think perhaps he thinks,
He is not strong and beautiful enough.

And yet his eyes are bluer than the heavens,
And full of such sweet light; and then his brow
Is like the brow of Dante which I saw
Once in a picture. Oh! he seems to me
To be the very noblest type of man.
Of late he has been gayer than his wont,
Playful, nay, almost merry, jesting oft,
Which is not like him, but it pleases me,
Though gayety is often but white foam,
Brief sparkles on the dark wine of despair.
Now he will be returning presently,
And I will lay my cheek against his arm,
As I have done in childhood. I will say,
'Dear Manley, I'm not worthy of your love,
And if you do not love me, tell me so;
But I shall love no other in the world.'
Then he will fold me close and kiss me long,
And all will then be well. O saucy moon,
How suddenly you stooped into a cloud,
And gathered all your light up from the world.
Ah! what a gust of wind! I think 'twill storm.
I'll close the window. Why does he not come?
Who knocks? A letter? Who should write to me?"

"I have been dreaming wild and foolish dreams.
Because my life was woven in with yours,
And all the threads so crossed and over-crossed,
That it were death to disentangle them,
I thought that we should marry, Magia.
And when the fortune came, you know I asked—
Do you remember?—'What if I were rich?'
Then all my blood ran rippling merrily.
I almost heard it singing in my veins.
But then the shadow that so many times

Had threatened me far off, approached, and fixed
Dread eyes of fire upon my soul, and said,
'Alas! how bright and beautiful she is!
As well the thistle marry with the rose.'
And so farewell, sweet Magia, my beloved!
I saw when Grandville held you to his breast,
And pressed a passionate kiss upon your lips.
I heard him speak to you in tender tones,
But would not seem to doubt by questioning.
Though testified against by every sense,
I should believe you noble, pure and true.
My will is in the little secret drawer.
You know the lock; you have the sister key.
I could not stay with you and hide my love,
And if you knew it, you might wrong yourself,
Being so kind and tender as you are.
I will not stand between you and your good.
Be happy, my belovèd; fare you well!"
A moment like a statue Magia stood,
Making no moan or outcry, being used
To suffer all things mutely.   Then she turned
And caught her mantle up and fled the house;
And Grandville, who was lingering by the door,
Demurring if to enter or pass on,
Followed her white robe like a flying cloud,
Until she stood upon the pier, and stretched
Her white arms toward the waves that swooped
    along,
Like giant birds of prey from some dead age,
Shaking their white plumes till the air was thick
With glistening down of spray, and then she cried,
"My heart is breaking, Manley!"

                              "Let it break!"
In thunder came the hollow answer back
From the mad, bounding billows, from far depths.

Her mantle streamed behind her in the wind
That tossed her dark curls wildly to and fro.
Her robes were drenched with sea-foam, still she
   stood
With outstretched arms, while Grandville vainly
   strove
To draw her thence, until at last she fell
Fainting upon her face, and then he raised
Her gently up, and staggering down the street,
Pressed with his burden through the night and
   storm.

Now when the beauteous lily of the light
Unfolded its white petals on the waves,
Revealing its sun-heart of gold, there came
The sound of heavy footsteps through the house,
And startled Magia from her swoon. She rose
And came to hear the heavy tidings. There,
All drenched with sea-foam, lay upon a chair,
His hat and coat, the linen handkerchief
Her patient hands had delicately wrought
With fine embroidery. "Alas!" said one,
"The hungry sea would have its sacrifice.
We could not save him, and, poor soul! he scarce
Had resolution for the deed. He stood
Long gazing in the roaring waves, then turned,
And thrice he moved away and thrice returned;
And when the light was breaking in the east,
He stretched his hands toward the wild sea and cried,
' My heart is breaking, Magia!' and leaped in.
We did not see him struggling in the waves,

So quickly they devoured him, but found
Only this hat and coat and handkerchief,
All drenched with sea-foam, lying on the pier.
His sister Magia comes.   Stand back! make way!"
She knelt, and on the garments laid her face
Buried in curls, but no one heard her words,
But knew she pleaded with him who was gone,
As if she thought his spirit lingered still
About its earthly garments, for they heard
Her piteous accents and sometimes his name.
Into her bosom's snowy drapery
Glided her hand and drew a picture forth.
And as she gazed, its blue eyes seemed to fill
With the sweet sorrow of all yearning love.
"I love you, Manley, I shall love none else
In all the world beside.   You do not speak.
Alas! you cannot, but I am your bride
From this hour and for all eternity.
Behold I seal our marriage covenant!"
She pressed her warm mouth to the pictured lips,
Then to the sea-wet garments many times.
All they who stood about her brushed the tears
That gathered on their lashes.   Magia
Wept not, but clasped the cold, wet garments close
Against her shivering bosom, kissing them.
At last, a strange light shining on her face,
She laid them by, and rising from her knees,
Passed from the room.   They fell back reverently,
Who stood about the threshold.   Grandville set
The door wide open for her feet to pass;
And like a ray of snowy moonlight marked,

Where the rich summer midnight of her hair
Met with the white dawn of her youthful brow,
A streak of silver. And he turned and wept.

PART IV

FREEDOM REGAINED

Right in the heart of sin and poverty,
Where Vice, unblushing and unvisored, walks
With his dark consort, Ignorance, up and down,
Quickly devouring up each little grain
Of virtue that dares sprout amid the filth,
Jeering at laws and laughing down reforms;
Here where the serfs of labor sometimes dream
Of being men and women some bright day
When they less hardly feel the cursèd grind
Of getting honest bread; here lifted up
The People's Institute its sober walls,
And asked the toiling populace to come
And taste a little of life's beautiful
In art and learning, in its galleries
And spacious libraries. And there, each day,
Were classes held in arts and sciences,
And learning's simplest rudiments, and there
Were weekly concerts free to every one,
That all might feel the grace of harmony.
For music, like an angel, gently moves
On the sweet pool of tears within the soul,
And troubles it unto its secret depths

With healing inspirations. Lectures too
Were given free to all, and once a week
Were social gatherings where all might come
And sit within the comfort and the peace
Of those bright, spacious rooms, and rest and chat.
Here oftentimes the toiling populace
Would come together, and in peaceful way
Discuss the evils of the social state,
The various remedies, how best applied;
And freely every individual spoke
Out the rude sense of justice in his soul.
This was the monument which Magia
Raised unto Manley's memory with the wealth
Bequeathed to her, and here she lived and worked,
And moved among the people like a light—
A star that quits its native firmament
And sister orbs, to wander through the gloom
Of unillumined spaces. Everywhere
Her footsteps came one dreamed that flowers sprang.
The children held their little faces up,
Smiling like blossoms turning to the sun
To catch the sunbeams. Angry eyes grew mild,
Hard faces softer, wrinkled brows more smooth,
In Magia's presence. So she lived and worked,
And never paled the rose upon her cheek,
As if, indeed, the sweet immortal soul
Immortalized the body; but the streak
Of silver on her forehead slowly grew,
Until the soft curls fell like drifted snow
About the gentle summer of her face.
There came a timid girl into the midst

Of the assembled people, on a night.
None turned his head or raised a curious eye,
But yet she blushed and shrank, and found a seat
By side of Magia, who gave her hand
In welcome. "Do I trespass?"
        "None does that
Who comes to us in faith and friendliness."
"You wish my name?"
       "No, not except you choose."
"Then call me simply Madeline, no more.
What are the people saying with such heat?"
"It is the social question which they moot.
One says, 'We are one family and the State
Should nurture us in fond maternal love,
Cherish the helpless and uphold the weak,
And lavish her abundance upon all
Impartially, like children she has borne.'
Another says, 'A tyrant is the State,
And laws but curse. Behold how they are mocked
And twisted, like a weathercock i' th' wind
Of every crazy brain that desecrates
The throne of Justice, sitting in pretense
Of the interpretation of the law,
But in the eyes of Justice blowing dust,
Meanwhile to prostitute the fairest laws
To personal, base ends. Down with the State!
Let each man follow out the natural law
Of his own being, and, amid the clash
Of human interests, and the daily shocks
Of conquest and defeat, the flash and fire
Of will smote hard on will, brain struck on brain—

Work out his highest individual good,
Giving mankind that noblest gift—a man.'
Another says, 'All wealth is from the land.
Give every man his birthright in the land,
Then will a vaster Eden come to earth
Than that whose white dews glimmered in the light
Of young creation's dawn.' Another says,
'Oh! let the old world spin around the sun,
And ripen when the golden season comes
For worlds to ripen. Let alone, I say.'"
"The man with snowy locks and burning eyes,
And flowing white beard, tell me, who is he?"
"He is a kind of prophet in our midst.
We call him Father, or the Nameless Man,
For so he calls himself. Hark to his words:
'None, none is free. It takes how vast a brain
To compass the whole thought of freedom! Lo,
Tyrants are slaves, not knowing they are so.
The rich have their peculiar bondage. Those,
Who do not cringe beneath some social lash,
Are oft in lowest serfdom to themselves.
O word of light upon the tongue of truth!
O tear of rapture in the eye of Love!
O marriage ring upon the strong white hand
Of most divinest Justice!—Liberty!
Thou angel leader of the centuries,
We see thy white wings strained against the dark
Of the far future, and thy starry locks
Clustered about thy temples, and thy mouth
A red rose glowing through the night, thy hand,
Like a white wand, still beckoning, beckoning.

Thou wilt not come to us, but we must haste
And follow after thee, and thou wilt lead
Us through the desert to a promised land
Where walk men's deeds like angels clothed in truth,
No cruel brand upon their foreheads white,
Made by the tiger claw of selfishness,
Their free wings rumpled by no fluttering
Against the cords of custom and of law.'
The fair, frail woman sitting at his side,
His daughter, is the people's nightingale.
They know her by no other name, and he
In speaking to her, always says: 'My Bird!'
And they two live and work among the poor,
She singing to the dying till they think
That seraphim float 'round them; to the sick
Not nigh to death, till soothed to healing sleep;
Unto the sad, and they are comforted:
So shares her rare gift freely with the throng."
Spoke Madeline, "I know her face. 'Tis she
Whose convict father, on a Christmas morn,
When all the bells were ringing merrily,
Her wedding chimes still echoing in her heart,
She being one month a bride, he having served
His prison sentence, came a suppliant.
She pleaded, but her husband shut the door
Upon him like a tramp, and after that
Remorse and secret grief made her cheek pale.
Whereat he grew suspicious, and he set
A watch upon her footsteps night and day,
Detected her in conference with a man,

Accused her. She protested earnestly
She only met her father; but he laughed.
Many believe she was a stainless wife,
As pure as snow before it falls from heaven,
And others say she was not wholly true
But she was driven and hounded into sin.
However it may have been, I know the court
Granted him his divorce, and took the child
Out of her arms, and gave it unto him,
And after that he never saw her more."
Said Magia softly, "Let no word of this
Be breathed in any other ear than mine.
The past is past; why should it leave its grave
To tread our present paths with haunting feet?
It takes the heart's whole strength to meet each hour
As it approaches; why should we give half
To combat with the ghosts of the dead years?
We ask of no one what his past has been,
But what his present is." Said Madeline,
"How many here have secrets in their eyes!
Their brows are palimpsests whereon are traced
Many strange records."
                    "Aye," said Magia,
"For every human life's a tragedy,
If but a Shakespeare or Euripides,
With glorifying touch, would lift it up
In the sweet light of sympathy which shows
All men its kindred touches unto all."
Then Madeline uplifted her fair face:
"I have grown very weary of myself,
And of the giddy world in which I move.

I pray you let me tarry here a while
And work with you."
      "Most welcome!" Magia said.
So for a week the gentle Madeline
Went up and down with Magia everywhere,
And drank her words and dwelt upon her ways.
Upon the evening of the seventh day
She came and flung herself at Magia's feet,
Crossing her gleaming arms on Magia's knees,
And over those white arms her auburn curls
Flashed down like rays of sunset, and through them
Her snowy fingers strayed caressingly.
"Am I not beautiful?"
       "Most beautiful,
And through the mortal beauty glows a mind,
And over all the glorifying grace
Of spirit beauty like a splendor falls."
Then Madeline made answer, drooping low,
"And yet one does not love me whom I love."
"Can you be sure of this? Have you been true?
Be sure no angel stands behind our deeds
To gather up the tangled ends we leave,
And weave them into beautiful designs!
These are the truest words of him *I* love."
Then Madeline drooped lower. "No," she said;
"For when they told me that he had gone wild
Over a beggar girl, a factory slave,
I would not hear him speak, nor even read
The letters that he sent me." Magia smiled:
"I am the beggar girl, the factory slave,
But we've not spoken alone for these three years.

He does me kindly service when he can,
Teaches the classes sometimes, sometimes speaks
Brave words unto the people, but I think
He has forgotten that fancy long ago."
Then Madeline drew down her thick, bright curls
Over her burning cheeks: "I did not know—
Forgive me, Magia, I did not know."
Magia, stooping, raised the drooping head,
Parted the sunset-colored ringlets back,
Kissing the fair brow: "Speak to him," she said.
"I fear me I shall seem unmaidenly."
"Fear nothing half so much as being untrue.
He comes again to-night; tell him the truth,
The simple truth, then let him go his way
And do his will; but speak the truth to him.
Oh! woman is too narrow, too bound in
By steels of custom, too opinion-laced.
Even in her fullest, fairest growth she shows
Some ugly twists where she has grown too cramped,
Some littlenesses that defeat her right
To the grave reverence of noble men,
Unfit her for great causes. Ask yourself,
Whate'er you do, 'Does reason sanction this?
Do I thus follow out my being's law,
Or serve a blind tradition?' Oh! I long
To see some splendid woman once attain
To all the fair proportions of a man,
His intellectual breadth, his passion's depth,
His height of courage and his strength of will;
Nor, in the fair unfolding of herself,
Miss aught of gracious sweetness; nor yet lose,

Through wisdom, the white bloom of innocence:
Snow pure, but not through ignorance of sin,
Or social screens set up to break the heat
Of fierce temptation's fires which men must face,
But through experience strong, through knowledge wise,
Spotless as heaven by conquest of herself."
Then Madeline made answer tremulously:
"No wonder that the children, when they pray,
Forget that it is God to whom they pray,
And lisp the name of Magia instead;
And the old men and women breathe the name
To charm away diseases; and the vile,
Who never yet have known a sense of shame,
Blush crimson in her presence; and no doubt,
Lovers will swear by her." Then Magia smiled:
"Oh! there are heavenly moments in our lives,
When sympathy makes angels of us all,
Clothing us with a mystic aureole;
And those whose sorrows have transfigured us
Seeing a light about us, kiss our robes,
And almost worship us, while other men
See nothing but unluminous, cold clay."
While she yet spoke, one stood within the room,
And seeing Grandville, Magia smiling passed
Out of the room in silence. Madeline
Rose from her lowly seat and moved toward him.
"Arthur!" she said; he answered, "Madeline!"
And they two looked into each other's eyes,
The while the noiseless footsteps of the light
Were stealing from the room. At last she drew

Herself unto her utmost queenly height,
Assuming a new dignity and strength,
Like a new royal robe: "I tell you true—
I have not ceased to love you in these years,
And I would know how is it now with you?"
He moved a little nearer, and knelt down,
And kissed her snowy fingers twice or thrice.
"You are as brave as you are beautiful,
As true as you are brave. Oh! I would bare
My forehead of its crown, were I a king,
Being so honored by the noble love
Of such a splendid woman. Yet if I say
That Magia is my heart's beloved, my star,
By which I shape the courses of my life,
The one true note by which my being tunes
Itself to the deep harmonies of life?—"
"Why then I would not have it otherwise.
No other is so worthy to be loved,"
She answered, faintly flushing. On that night,
The lecture finished, all the people pressed
To touch the hand of Magia ere they went;
And when the last had gone, the last but one,
And they two stood within the empty hall,
He touched her hand, all reverent as the rest:
"I have been keeping silent, Magia,
Till I could grow up slowly to your height
Of moral greatness, struggling day by day
To fashion something nobler of myself.
My cheek is scorched with burning shame to think
How weak and base you know me to have been,
Yet I have more to utter of myself,

Ere I am free to say the thing I must,
More that I faint to breathe to one Christ-pure."
"Speak truly, but speak chastely, for believe
That truth and purity may lover-like
Walk hand in hand together through all speech,
Aye, through all thought and action, never divorced
Save in the thought of man and by his will."
"Oh! then, there are dark places in my life,
For there's a social license given to men,
Ruthless to trail the virginal white robes
Of their affections in the social slime."
"The past is past; why call it from its grave
To haunt the present?" Magia softly said.
"I say to you that I have sometimes stood
In presence of unblushing, naked sin,
And laid my hand upon its beating heart,
And analyzed its pulses, and I know
That that which is most God-like in a man
May make him most a fiend, as the same force
Which in the lurid lightning blasts the oak,
And fells the strong man sheltered under it,
In the brave hand of Science makes the night
Almost the radiant sister of the day.
So that which made us demons yesterday,
To-day may make us angels, if we will."
"Then, Magia, have I leave to speak of love,
Having concealed aught of myself from you?"
"Oh! I am married, Arthur, married! Why!
You would not seek to woo another's bride?"
"Married!" he said; "I scarcely understand."
"Yes, married, for I hold that when two hearts

Stand up together in the light of truth,
Before the rosy altar-fires of love,
Amid their pulses' music loud and sweet,
Like angel orchestras and wedding bells,
Confessing each to each, 'We truly love,'—
This is the marriage moment; this the act.
What more can form or ceremony add?
And all earth's forms and rituals cannot make
That marriage where this hath not been; and they,
Who deem that they are wedded by mere rites,
But live unchastely, out of marriage. Some
May think that death dissolves the marriage tie;
Indissoluble it makes it unto me,
For while life is, there may be death of love,
But after death love has no power to die."
"Oh! it was you who saved me, Magia."
"No, no, salvation is within a man—
A deathless spark at center of the soul,
That any breath of love or truth may fan
Into a splendor unimprisonable,
Illumining and quickening the whole man."
He bowed his head in sorrow: "I can wait."

The years rushed by, the tireless, swift years,
And made no change in Magia, save to turn
The white curls whiter, like soft drifted snow.
And Madeline dwelt with her, drinking in
Her pure soul's strength and sweetness, as a flower
Follows the sun with thirsty anthers. Now
Was Magia's early sorrow ten years old.
Upon its birthday morn she robed herself

In bridal white, and sat alone, and held
Some humble poet's volume in her hand.
She read aloud, aloud, though to herself,
A quivering, far-off sweetness in her voice,
As when a sweet-tongued clock down some long aisle
Throbs lingering music, like an angel hid
Amid the shadows, singing to himself.
Now Arthur Grandville, not remembering
What day it was, came with a purpose firm
To say, "See, I have waited patiently.
Dear Magia, I am content to take
Love's blossom of the later spring." He stood
Within the door. Her face being turned from him
She knew not of his presence, and read on:

"O Yesterday, sad Yesterday, return
And be a willing bride to this To-day
With all its fuller knowledge, and behold
The beautiful To-morrow—the bright birth,
Fair issue of this noble marriage. Oh!
Yet our mistakes are angels, if we throne
Them in our hearts, and sitting at their feet,
Learn meekly all the wisdom they can teach."
She slowly turned the leaves and once more read:

"Sleep on thy white cloud pillows, O sweet wind,
And whisper of thy wanderings in thy sleep.
See yonder the white eyelids of the dawn
Tremble their dewy lashes and close down
Over their starry orbs, as the day comes,
Veiling the morning stars with stronger light.

I'm weary, for, through all the starful night,
My soul has reached forth the strong arm of thought
And searched about the world for truth, pure truth.
Once did my fingers close upon the hem
Of her white garment, and I felt the thrill
Of her electric being through me run.
I laughed for joy, when, lo! she fled my touch.
And once, oh, joy! I caught her, held her fast,
And lover-like I strained her to my soul.
She looked up into my soul's eyes and smiled,
A calm, compassionate, half disdainful smile.
She said, 'O soul, what wilt thou do with me?
Make me a robe of perishable words,
And show me to thy scoffing race? Knowest not
That when this new age, being fully ripe,
Shall drop into Time's palm and have its wine
Pressed out by his strong fingers, many things
Men hold as truth will be disproved, undone,
Only the wine, the spirit essence left?
Then shall I stand of words disgarmented,
Leaning in naked glory upon God.
I tell thee each must seek me for himself.
Nathless, if thou wilt have me bide with thee,
Thou must mount higher, nearer to God's throne,
Nor faint nor falter.' So she spoke, and slipped
Forth like a shining shadow. After her
My soul kept following hard, and passed at length
Into a realm of dim abstraction, where
Are awful glooms and mighty leaps of thought.
And there it grew confused and missed its way,
Yet struggled onward, shivering with doubt,

Like a scared angel stumbling 'gainst the stars,
Jostled to right and left by rushing worlds.
On, on and up, forever on and up,
Through shadowy wonders, tangled lights and darks,
Through labyrinths of nebulous star-shapes,
Ethereal essence upon essence heaped.
On, on and up, forever on and up,
Truth's silver footfall tinkling just above.
She passed within the circle of God's throne.
My soul, recoiling, veiled its dazzled eyes,
And prayed 'Come forth to me, O blessed Truth!'
With bended brows that could not be upraised,
Because of that great weight of glory, prayed,
'Daughter of God, come forth.' And presently
She came, with her grand head inclining low,
To kiss my soul's dropped eyelids, strengthening
　　them.
She led it back into the world of sense.
Straightway I fell to work with feverish zeal
To make a robe of subtly woven words
With which to clothe her limbs. When it was done,
And from her shoulders fell in graceful sweeps,
I held her from me, gazing long. She smiled,
A calm, compassionate, half-disdainful smile,
And cried, 'Lo, thou hast won me for thyself.
But though thou sing a song so strong and sweet
That it were worthy to be sung in heaven,
And thou shouldst sit beneath the evening star
And hear some seraph warbling that same song,
As Theban Pindar heard the great god Pan
Singing a mortal ode of his, and smiled

In voiceless rapture; and though other men
Should take your song of truth upon their lips,
And nimbly jingle it from tongue to tongue,
Yet would it not be theirs without the strife,
The strong, persistent struggle of the years
That wins the truth, a salt into the blood,
A tissue in the being's tissues. Yea,
I say that none shall have me for his own,
Except he follow me as thou hast done.'
Now I behold the pensive, dewy earth
With a long sweep of flowing sunlight dries
Her dewy lashes, rises up and goes
A-singing to her work. I rise and go,
Believing I have only slept and dreamed,
Yet having gained some wisdom out of dreams."
Once more she turned the leaves and once more
    read:

"All social schemes, like embryo infants, lie
In the vast evolution of the world,
Beneath its mighty heart, whose thunder-throbs
Are the world-shaking centuries. Let them grow,
Unfolding slowly, ripening to their hour.
To force them to their birth is certain death.
But nourish the great mother with the wine
Pressed from the fruit of ripe experience;
Make her blood rich with wisdom; let the sun
Of science shine upon her; let her breathe
The calm, pure air of reason, till at last
Unimportuned she will present the world
With its sublimest social dream fulfilled."

He heard the quivering sweetness of her voice,
And felt himself abashed, as if he stood
In presence of an angel strayed from heaven,
Whom one might worship, but not marry. Then
She turned a little way, and Grandville saw
A picture 'twixt the pages of her book.
He knew the white breadth of the thought-stretched
    brow,
The meek fire of the beautiful, mild eyes,
The mouth's grave sweetness, and he bowed his head
In reverential sorrow, would have passed
Out swiftly, noiselessly, but Magia felt
Rather than saw him there, and turned and smiled,
And beckoned to him. Arthur came and sat
Upon a footstool low at Magia's feet.
Then Magia softly said, "If I should die—"
"What then were life to me?"
                            "If I should die—"
"Oh! do not speak of death."
                            "If I should die,
I leave this work to you and Madeline.
Here in this splendid city by the lake,
I dream that man has a majestic hope,
Because all elements of life and thought
Enrich her blood and stimulate her brain.
Here is the world epitomized, for here
Are pulses out of every nation's heart,
And men may study mankind at their hearths.
This is to be a favorite battle-ground
For truth and error. Here, as time moves on,
Great causes will be marshaled. Times have been

Already when the stirring trumpet blast
Of an approaching conflict shook the world
Out of its dream of safety. Oh! then teach
All capable of bearing the bright arms
Of reason, fearless, independent thought.
If you would lead men surely angelward,
 Teach them to think,—not what to think, but how.
I fear me that the tendency of man
Is backward and not forward, down, not up.
But for a white-winged instinct in his soul,
Impelling him to strive against the things
Which drag him bruteward, he would sink again
Into the ape and tiger. Oh, how long
It takes to move the whole, great world an inch,
The whole, great world together! As for me,
I am a-weary of the heat and din
Of the perpetual warfare. If I lie
Down like a wounded soldier in his tent,
And slumber, will you carry on the siege
'Gainst sin and ignorance?" He simply said,
"The cause is truth, the lifting up of men,
The lighting of the world, your cause and mine."
She rose up then, complaining weariness,
But smiling still, and with the lightest touch
Of lips upon his forehead, left him there,
Still as a breathing statue, one long hour.

Soon there arose a tumult through the house,
The sound of hurrying feet and closing doors.
As swift as hungry fire through withered leaves,
From lip to lip the mournful message ran,

That Magia was dying. How they thronged
About the doors and through the rooms and halls,
The ragged children sobbing, and the men
And women, with their homely garments thick
With honest grime and odors of their toil,
Sobbing like children; those who, stained by crime,
Touching that pure and perfect life, had grown
More nearly pure and perfect; hearts made hard
And sour through man's injustice, that her smile
Mellowed and sweetened, knowing she had bent
Her young head to the biting, wintry wind
Of inhumanity, still uncongealed
Keeping the warm, sweet fountains of her heart.
The street was darkened by a sea of heads
That ever swayed and murmured, now and then
Sending a loud, hoarse moan up, as the word
Was passed along that Magia would die.
The wind blew and the rain fell on their heads,
And still they stood and shivered hour by hour.
A stranger forced his passage through the throng,
A man with sunburned cheeks and mild blue eyes.
At edge of the brown hair there gleamed a streak
Of delicate white skin, where the broad-rimmed hat
Had foiled the passionate kisses of the sun.
He was not tall enough nor straight enough
For perfect physical beauty, but he wore
An air of gracious dignity and strength
About him, as of one who, once for all,
Has laid a master hand upon himself.
Nor was there wanting manly thews of limb,
Nor the warm flush of health upon the cheek.

Breathless he pushed his way amid the crowd,
With gentle rudeness thrust the children by,
And all who would restrain him, till he came
Where Grandville, standing sentinel at the stairs,
Kept back the anxious throng. "You must not
    pass."
"I must, for I must see her. Will she die?"
"She will."
            "She *shall* not."
                    "Aye, I think she will,
As some rare rose, in full and perfect bloom,
That stands the season's storms, untimely frosts
And all prevailing blights, and shows no flaw,
Then suddenly upon a still, fair day,
Sheds all at once its petals, and is gone.
But who are you?"
            "One who may bring her help."
"A new physician?"
              "Aye, and one that brings
An unknown remedy. Pray let me pass."
He pressed on unresisted, till he stood
In Magia's chamber, where she lay and smiled,
Her eyelids shut, like delicate curtains drawn
On luminous windows. And as one who turns
His back upon the sun that he may look
Down some long, shadowy vista, Magia seemed
To gaze far backward, murmuring as she gazed,
That quivering, far-off sweetness in her voice:
"Lean on me, little brother. I am strong.
I'll hold my cloak around you. How the sleet
Pricks in the face like needles! Thank you, sir;

He is my brother, and we must have work
Together. Ah! the sun is shining bright.
You feed the swans. There's only a few crumbs.
You like to feed them, and I like to watch
Them stretch their red beaks. Brother, when we're rich
We'll buy some water lilies just like those."

All day the rain had fallen heavily,
And the low thunder moaned about the sky,
And the wind grieved from street to street; but now
A sea of crimson glory filled the west,
Arched by a rainbow bright as angel dreams,
Above which rolled the storm-clouds, thridded through
With lightning threads that ran and counter-ran,
As if an angel, holding in his hand,
A needle threaded with a silver thread,
Were mending the rent mantle of the storm.
Then Magia turned her eyelids toward the west,
And with uplifted finger cried, "Behold!
An angel stands on yonder sunset cloud,
A rainbow on his forehead. It is he!"
The stranger knelt. None understood his words,
But knew he pleaded with her, for they heard
His piteous accents, and sometimes her name.
She, thinking that the angel in the cloud
Was speaking to her, stretched her hands and cried,
"He beckons to me; he is speaking. Lo,
His tones are sweeter than they were on earth,
As angels' should be. Brother, I will come!"

She stretched both hands toward the bright sunset-
    cloud.
"O Magia," the stranger cried aloud,
Clasping her outstretched hands in wild despair,
"Help! help! Your brother needs you, Magia!
I die except you save me, Magia!
Will you not stay and help me, Magia?"
Slowly she turned her sweet, bewildered face,
And gazed into his beautiful, mild eyes.
"O Magia, I have returned alive,
I am not dead, although I meant to die,
Up to the very moment. Then there came
A wiser thought, touched with a gleam of hope—
To go away, and let you think me dead
For ten long years, so leave you free to choose.
And so I left my garments on the pier,
To carry the false message unto you,
And in the dawning's darkness crept away,
And journeyed to a far-off land, and there
I lived and worked beneath a tropic sun,
And gathered health of body and peace of mind.
These ten years being past, I set my face
Toward home and Magia, all my senses whet
Unto a twofold keenness. I could hear
The timid pulses in the veins of flowers,
The dazed stars tripping on the robes of dawn,
The soft wing-music of the passing hours,
Strange melody from spheres beyond our own,
The low-toned planets, and the flute-like wail
Of patient suns that feed their worlds with light
Through linked forevers. I could see the eve

Distilling its bright dews far up in heaven.
I saw the sun and ocean making clouds,
The opening of new buds, the birth of worlds;
And yet, through all my journey's weary length,
The glory of her smile was everywhere,
Clothing the whole world with an aureole.
The music of her voice was everywhere,
Girdling the world with melody. I seemed
To hear her calling to me night and day,
'Hasten, my brother! Oh! make haste!' I tried
To warn my heart against too wild a hope,
Lest it should bring too wild despair. I said,
'Alas! she may be dead, perchance be wed!'
But still my soul was jubilant, and came
Swift as a bridegroom certain of his bride.
You cannot die and leave me in the world.
You must not, will not, Magia!"
        "No," she said.
"Then we are married, married, Magia.
Behold we seal our marriage covenant."
He laid his warm, red lips against her own,
And in the kiss-long rapture of that breath
Was all of life to him, of life to her.

CONCLUSION

The autumn day was almost done. The lake
Was at its stillest, and the sun was low.
Two little boats rocked gently on the waves
Near to each other. Madeline laid by

Her dripping oar, and lifted up her face,—
Ripe cheeks that tempt the rich, red lips of youth,
White forehead with a nimbus of bright hair,—
And speaking to her fellow oarsman, said,
"See how the sunlight gleams on Magia's curls!
Oh, that I were like her—so strong and sweet!"
Then Arthur too laid by his oar and said:
"Sometimes a solstice in the soul's year comes,
When in its calm, high spheres its great lights
    pause,
While lower elements tempestuous rage,
And then move on serenely, calm, but changed,
For a new season has been ushered in.
So was it my soul's solstice on the day
When young Marcellus from the grave returned.
Then a new season reigned. Then I beheld
What heights of spiritual life had risen
Between my soul and Magia's; how she moved
Too far above me, like the moon in heaven,
In calm, pure splendor, while I, like the sea,
Yearned far below in passionate unrest.
But I will love her still, and love her well,
As loves the sea, the moon, far off, far off—
As man might love an angel. But for you,
You who are like her in all gracious ways,
In gentle truth and sweet sincerity,
You are my earthly Magia whom I dare
To love and marry. Answer if I may."
"I am content," she answered, "to be loved
Because I am like Magia." Then they heard
A sudden chord of music from the lips

Of Magia and Manley, a brief pulse
Of laughter. He had raised a snowy curl
That gleamed on Magia's shoulder, to his lips.
"It is more beautiful than when it wore
Its richest midnight luster."
                          "Ah!" she said,
"A little life's how slight a thing! It falls,
And like a snowflake slips into the sea,
And melts from sight; and yet what costly things—
Tears, anguish, passions, dreams, wrongs, battles,
    blood,—
It takes to make a strong, true life that feels
All human nature conquered in the blood!
Men are so bound, and yet so wide apart!
Together by what mighty likeness held!
Yet, by what differences immeasurable,
What gulfs impassable, oft separate!
So one may move a stranger in the throng,
Feeling he has no kindred in the world,
Yet, yearning, knows that all men are his kin.
So when I thought you were not in the world,
I seemed a stranger, brother." How he smiled!
"Who is it calls me brother? What!—my wife?
These ivy vines of habit, how they cling
About our thoughts and actions, creeping in
Amid the careless words that shape our speech,
Binding us to the ruins of the past
That else might crumble from us." Then they two
Struck a low chord of laughter, thrilled and sweet,
Which throbbed an instant on the wind, then fell
Into the blue waves, fading out of sound.

Now, like a golden period from the pen
Of Time, the ancient scrivener, the great sun
Fell on the shining surface of the lake,
And left the western sky all glorious
With tints innumerable, as if it were
The gathering place of souls of earth's dead flowers.
Spoke Manley: "Let our chiefest mission be,
To make ourselves the noblest that we may;
And second, to ennoble other men;
Because the great Christ-passion to redeem
Burns in our hearts, and life is but half lived,
Unless we feel that men have touched our robes,
And virtue has gone out from us."
                                    "And yet,"
Said Magia, gazing thoughtfully, "and yet,
I do not like this clang of forging men,
Like white hot iron at our social forge.
I think salvation is within a man,
A deathless spark at center of his soul,
That outward burns; and they who beat the drums
Of progress, and ring out the wild alarms
Of death and danger, oft confuse the world.
And yet, we may not live unto ourselves.
How shall we serve the world best?   Let us think."

www.ingramcontent.com/pod-product-compliance
Lightning Source LLC
Chambersburg PA
CBHW020827190426
43197CB00037B/724